HMH | (into) Reading™

my Book 1

Authors and Advisors

Alma Flor Ada • Kylene Beers • F. Isabel Campoy
Joyce Armstrong Carroll • Nathan Clemens
Anne Cunningham • Martha C. Hougen
Elena Izquierdo • Carol Jago • Erik Palmer
Robert E. Probst • Shane Templeton • Julie Washington

Contributing Consultants

David Dockterman • Mindset Works®
Jill Eggleton

Welcome to myBook!

Do you like to read different kinds of texts for all kinds of reasons? Do you have a favorite genre or author? What can you learn from a video? Do you think carefully about what you read and view?

Here are some tips to get the MOST out of what you read and view:

Set a Purpose. What is the title? What is the genre? What do you want to learn from this text or video? What about it looks interesting to you?

Read and Annotate. As you read, underline and highlight important words and ideas. Make notes about things you want to figure out or remember. What questions do you have? What are your favorite parts? Write them down!

Make Connections. How does the text or video connect to what you already know? To other texts or videos? To your own life or community? Talk to others about your ideas. Listen to their ideas, too.

Wrap It Up! Look back at your questions and annotations. What did you like best? What did you learn? What do you still want to know? How will you find out?

As you read the texts and watch the videos in this book, make sure you get the MOST out of them by using the tips above.

But, don't stop there . . . Decide what makes you curious, find out more about it, have fun, and never stop learning!

5

MODULE 2

Come to Your Senses

SCIENCE CONNECTION: Using the Senses **98**

Performance Task

MODULE 3

Rise to the Occasion

MODULE 5

Art Everywhere

What Makes Us Who We Are?

"Experience is the teacher of all things."

— Julius Caesar

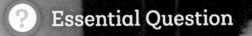

Essential Question

How do your experiences help shape your identity?

Words About Who We Are

The words in the chart will help you talk and write about the selections in this module. Which words about your experiences have you seen before? Which words are new to you?

Add to the Vocabulary Network on page 13 by writing synonyms, antonyms, and related words and phrases for each word about who we are.

After you read each selection in this module, come back to the Vocabulary Network and keep building it. Add more ovals if you need to.

WORD	MEANING	CONTEXT SENTENCE
identity (noun)	Your identity is who you are.	My love of sports is part of my identity.
experience (noun)	Your experience is made up of past events and feelings.	Meeting my favorite author is an experience I will never forget.
wisdom (noun)	If you have wisdom, you are able to use your experience to make good decisions.	Our grandmother, who is full of wisdom, always gives us good advice.
pursuit (noun)	A pursuit is something you attempt to accomplish.	In our pursuit of the science fair trophy, we worked after school every day for a month.

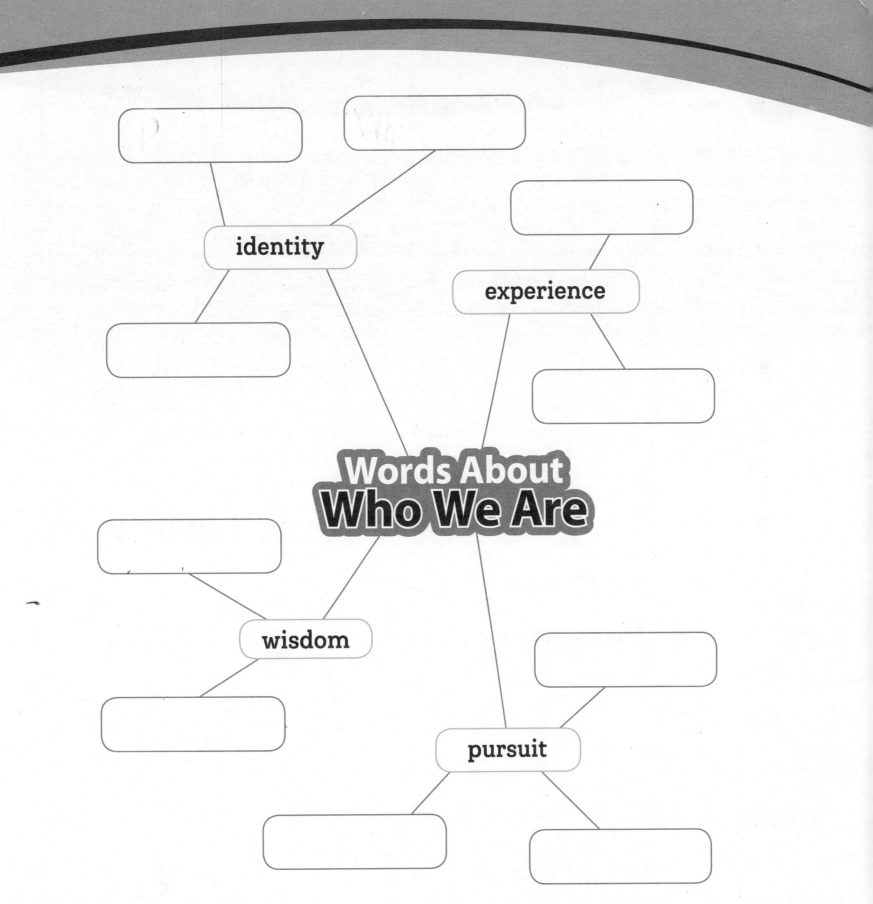

identity

experience

**Words About
Who We Are**

wisdom

pursuit

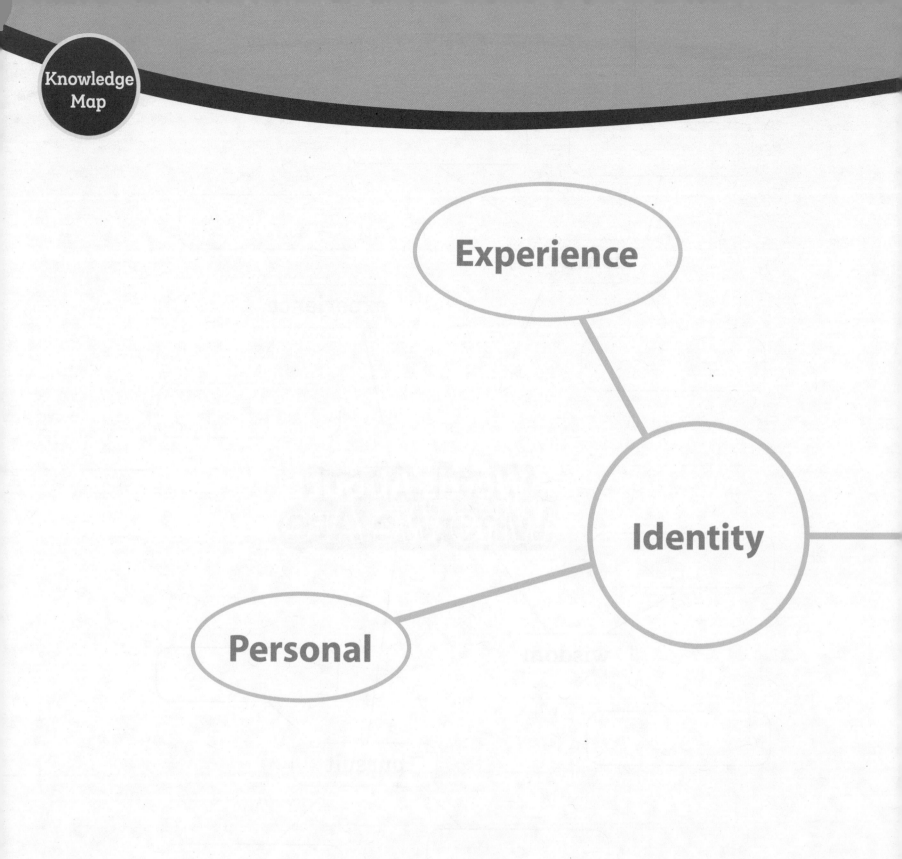

Experience

Identity

Personal

Cultural

The Story of You

1   Have you ever felt like you are a character in a book? Well, in some ways, you are. In fact, you are *THE* main character in a story. It's the story of your life. If it were made into a book, it could be called *The Story of You*.

2   So, what shapes the "you" in *The Story of You*? Well, just like in any story, it's the people, places, and events that surround you. It's also your own ideas, beliefs, and actions. All of these are the influences that shape you, give you your identity, and make you the unique character you are.

³ Characters

Your family and friends are the other characters in your story. They start to shape you as soon as you are born. These people share their wisdom, laugh at your jokes, and tell you their own stories and secrets.

⁴ Events

The events in your story are always shaping you. These are the experiences you have as you live your life. They include all of your interests and the pursuits that you follow by yourself, or with family.

5 Settings

The settings in your story are the places you live in and pass through. School teaches you how and what to learn. Your neighborhood puts you in touch with adults doing different jobs. These places expose you to different ideas, traditions, and points of view.

6 **Think about the characters, settings, and events in your life. Then, tell someone the story of you!**

Notice & Note
Aha Moment

Prepare to Read

GENRE STUDY ▸ A **fantasy** is an imaginative story with characters and events that are not real.

- Authors of fantasies tell the story through the plot, or the main events of the story.

- Fantasy stories may include illustrations that describe the characters and setting and may give clues about the plot.

- Some fantasy stories are set in the real world, but the characters might have unusual abilities.

SET A PURPOSE ▸ **Look at** the pictures in the selection. What do you notice about the girl in the story? What would you like to learn about her? Write your ideas below.

Meet the Author:
Kate DiCamillo
Meet the Illustrator:
K.G. Campbell

CRITICAL VOCABULARY

cynic

defiance

profound

inadvertently

consumed

descended

obliged

mundane

considered

disdain

Flora & Ulysses

The Illuminated Adventures

BY
KATE DiCAMILLO

ILLUSTRATED BY
K.G. CAMPBELL

1   *F*lora Belle Buckman was in her room at her desk. She was very busy. She was doing two things at once. She was ignoring her mother, and she was also reading a comic book entitled *The Illuminated Adventures of the Amazing Incandesto!*

2   "Flora," her mother shouted, "what are you doing up there?"

3   "I'm reading!" Flora shouted back.

4   "Remember the contract!" her mother shouted. "Do not forget the contract!"

5   At the beginning of summer, in a moment of weakness, Flora had made the mistake of signing a contract that said she would "work to turn her face away from the idiotic high jinks of comics and toward the bright light of true literature."

6   Those were the exact words of the contract. They were her mother's words.

7   Flora's mother was a writer. She was divorced, and she wrote romance novels.

8   Talk about idiotic high jinks.

9   Flora hated romance novels.

10   In fact, she hated romance.

11   "I hate romance," said Flora out loud to herself. She liked the way the words sounded. She imagined them floating above her in a comic-strip bubble; it was a comforting thing to have words hanging over her head. Especially negative words about romance.

I HATE ROMANCE.

24

12   Flora's mother had often accused Flora of being a "natural-born cynic."

13   Flora suspected that this was true.

SHE WAS A NATURAL-BORN CYNIC WHO LIVED IN DEFIANCE OF CONTRACTS!

14   *Yep,* thought Flora, *that's me.* She bent her head and went back to reading about the amazing Incandesto.

15   She was interrupted a few minutes later by a very loud noise.

16   It sounded as if a jet plane had landed in the Tickhams' backyard.

17   "What the heck?" said Flora. She got up from her desk and looked out the window and saw Mrs. Tickham running around the backyard with a shiny, oversize vacuum cleaner.

18   It looked like she was vacuuming the yard.

19   *That can't be,* thought Flora. *Who vacuums their yard?*

20   Actually, it didn't look like Mrs. Tickham knew *what* she was doing.

21   It was more like the vacuum cleaner was in charge. And the vacuum cleaner seemed to be out of its mind. Or its engine. Or something.

22   "A few bolts shy of a load," said Flora out loud.

23   And then she saw that Mrs. Tickham and the vacuum cleaner were headed directly for a squirrel.

cynic   A cynic is someone who always expects bad things to happen.

defiance   If you act in defiance, you know something is not allowed, but you do it anyway.

24 "Hey, now," said Flora.

25 She banged on the window.

26 "Watch out!" she shouted. "You're going to vacuum up that squirrel!"

27 She said the words, and then she had a strange moment of seeing them, hanging there over her head.

"YOU'RE GOING TO VACUUM UP THAT SQUIRREL!"

28 *There is just no predicting what kind of sentences you might say,* thought Flora. *For instance, who would ever think you would shout, "You're going to vacuum up that squirrel!"?*

29 It didn't make any difference, though, what words she said. Flora was too far away. The vacuum cleaner was too loud. And also, clearly, it was bent on destruction.

30 "This malfeasance must be stopped," said Flora in a deep and superheroic voice.

31 "This malfeasance must be stopped" was what the unassuming janitor Alfred T. Slipper always said before he was transformed into the amazing Incandesto and became a towering, crime-fighting pillar of light.

32 Unfortunately, Alfred T. Slipper wasn't present.

33 Where was Incandesto when you needed him?

34 Not that Flora really believed in superheroes. But still.

35 She stood at the window and watched as the squirrel was vacuumed up.

36 *Poof. Fwump.*

37 "Holy bagumba," said Flora.

38 𝒩ot much goes on in the mind of a squirrel.

39 Huge portions of what is loosely termed "the squirrel brain" are given over to one thought: food.

40 The average squirrel cogitation goes something like this: *I wonder what there is to eat.*

41 This "thought" is then repeated with small variations (e.g., *Where's the food? Man, I sure am hungry. Is that a piece of food?* and *Are there more pieces of food?*) some six or seven thousand times a day.

42 All of this is to say that when the squirrel in the Tickhams' backyard got swallowed up by the Ulysses 2000X, there weren't a lot of terribly profound thoughts going through his head.

43 As the vacuum cleaner roared toward him, he did not (for instance) think, *Here, at last, is my fate come to meet me!*

44 He did not think, *Oh, please, give me one more chance and I will be good.*

45 What he thought was, *Man, I sure am hungry.*

46 And then there was a terrible roar, and he was sucked right off his feet.

47 At that point, there were no thoughts in his squirrel head, not even thoughts of food.

profound A profound thought is one that is deep and meaningful.

48 **S**eemingly, swallowing a squirrel was a bit much even for the powerful, indomitable, indoor/outdoor Ulysses 2000X. Mrs. Tickham's birthday machine let out an uncertain roar and stuttered to a stop.

49 Mrs. Tickham bent over and looked down at the vacuum cleaner.

50 There was a tail sticking out of it.

51 "For heaven's sake," said Mrs. Tickham, "what next?"

52 She dropped to her knees and gave the tail a tentative tug.

53 She stood. She looked around the yard.

54 "Help," she said. "I think I've killed a squirrel."

55 **F**lora ran from her room. She ran down the stairs. As she ran, she thought, *For a cynic, I am a surprisingly helpful person.*

56 She went out the back door.

57 Her mother called to her. She said, "Where are you going, Flora Belle?"

58 Flora didn't answer her. She never answered her mother when she called her Flora Belle.

59 Sometimes she didn't answer her mother when she called her Flora, either.

60   Flora ran through the tall grass and cleared the fence between her yard and the Tickhams' in a single bound.

61   "Move out of the way," said Flora. She gave Mrs. Tickham a shove and grabbed hold of the vacuum cleaner. It was heavy. She picked it up and shook it. Nothing happened. She shook harder. The squirrel dropped out of the vacuum cleaner and landed with a *plop* on the grass.

62   He didn't look that great.

63   He was missing a lot of fur. Vacuumed off, Flora assumed.

64   His eyelids fluttered. His chest rose and fell and rose again. And then it stopped moving altogether.

65   Flora knelt. She put a finger on the squirrel's chest.

66   At the back of each issue of *The Illuminated Adventures of the Amazing Incandesto!* there was a series of bonus comics. One of Flora's very favorite bonus comics was entitled *TERRIBLE THINGS CAN HAPPEN TO YOU!* As a cynic, Flora found it wise to be prepared. Who knew what horrible, unpredictable thing would happen next?

67 *TERRIBLE THINGS CAN HAPPEN TO YOU!*
detailed what action to take if you inadvertently
consumed plastic fruit (this happened more often
than you would suppose—some plastic fruit was
extremely realistic looking); how to perform the
Heimlich maneuver on your elderly aunt Edith if she
choked on a stringy piece of steak at an all-you-can-
eat buffet; what to do if you were wearing a striped
shirt and a swarm of locusts descended (run: locusts
eat stripes); and, of course, how to administer
everyone's favorite lifesaving technique: CPR.

68 *TERRIBLE THINGS CAN HAPPEN TO YOU!*
did not, however, detail exactly how someone was
supposed to give CPR to a squirrel.

inadvertently   If you act inadvertently, you do something by mistake or without realizing it.

consumed   If you consumed something, you ate it.

descended   If something descended, it moved downwards.

69   "I'll figure it out," said Flora.

70   "What will you figure out?" said Mrs. Tickham.

71   Flora didn't answer her. Instead, she bent down and put her mouth on the squirrel's mouth.

72   It tasted funny.

73   If she were forced to describe it, she would say that it tasted exactly like squirrel: fuzzy, damp, slightly nutty.

74   "Have you lost your mind?" said Mrs. Tickham.

75   Flora ignored her.

76   She breathed into the squirrel's mouth. She pushed down on his small chest.

77   She started to count.

---

78 ***B***reathe!

79 The squirrel obliged. He took a deep, shuddering breath. And then another. And another.

80   The squirrel returned.

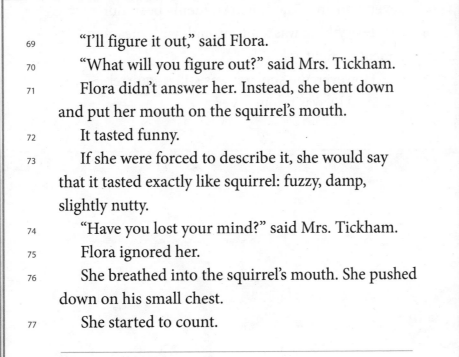

obliged   If you obliged, you did what you were asked or expected to do.

81 **T**he squirrel was a little unsteady on his feet.

82 His brain felt larger, roomier. It was as if several doors in the dark room of his self (doors he hadn't even known existed) had suddenly been flung wide.

83 Everything was shot through with meaning, purpose, light.

84 However, the squirrel was still a squirrel.

85 And he was hungry. Very.

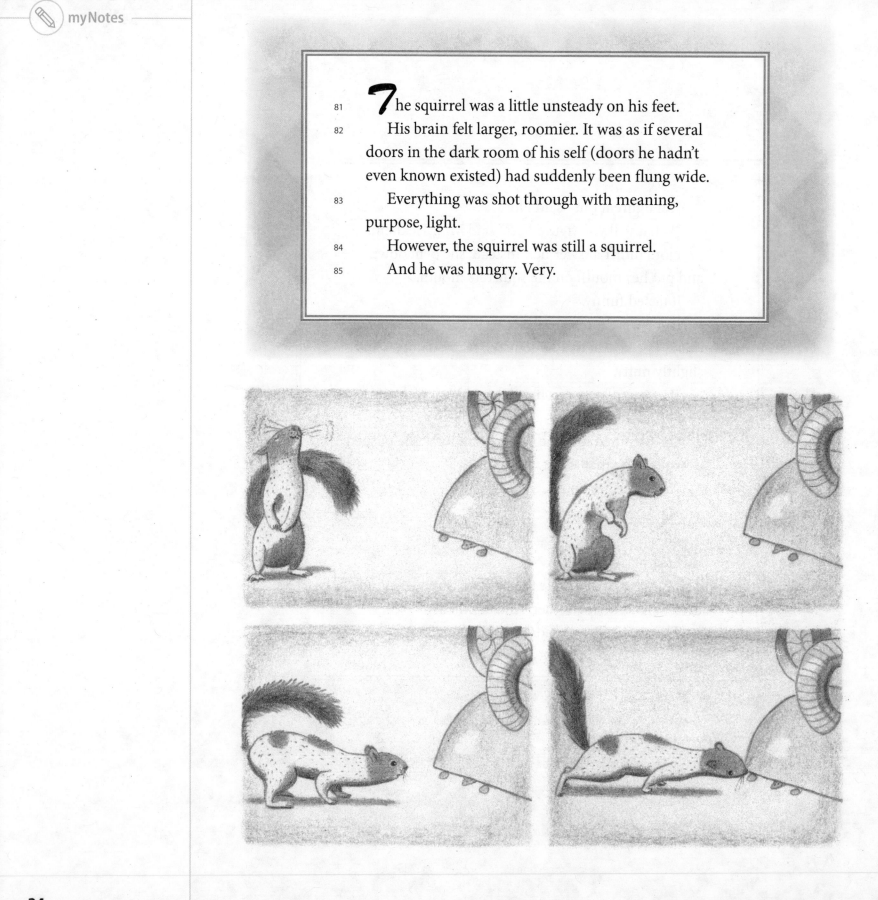

mundane   Someone who is mundane is ordinary and often dull.

86   *F*lora and Mrs. Tickham noticed at the same time.

87   "The squirrel," said Flora.

88   "The vacuum cleaner," said Mrs. Tickham.

89   Together, they stared at the Ulysses 2000X and at the squirrel, who was holding it over his head with one paw.

90   "That can't be," said Mrs. Tickham.

91   The squirrel shook the vacuum cleaner.

92   "That can't be," said Mrs. Tickham.

93   "You already said that," said Flora.

94   "I'm repeating myself?"

95   "You're repeating yourself."

96   "Maybe I have a brain tumor," said Mrs. Tickham.

97   It was certainly possible that Mrs. Tickham had a brain tumor. Flora knew from reading *TERRIBLE THINGS CAN HAPPEN TO YOU!* that a surprising number of people were walking around with tumors in their brains and didn't even know it. That was the thing about tragedy. It was just sitting there, keeping you company, waiting. And you had absolutely no idea.

98   This was the kind of helpful information you could get from the comics if you paid attention.

99   The other kind of information that you absorbed from the regular reading of comics (most particularly from the regular reading of *The Illuminated Adventures of the Amazing Incandesto!*) was that impossible things happened all the time.

100   For instance, heroes—superheroes—were born of ridiculous and unlikely circumstances: spider bites, chemical spills, planetary dislocation, and, in the case of Alfred T. Slipper, from accidental submersion in an industrial-size vat of cleaning solution called Incandesto! (The Cleaning Professional's Hardworking Friend).

101   "I don't think you have a brain tumor," said Flora. "There might be another explanation."

102   "Uh-huh," said Mrs. Tickham. "What's the other explanation?"

103   "Have you ever heard of Incandesto?"

104   "What?" said Mrs. Tickham.

105   "Who," said Flora. "Incandesto is a who. He's a superhero."

106   "Right," said Mrs. Tickham. "And your point is?"

107   Flora raised her right hand. She pointed with a single finger at the squirrel.

108   "Surely you're not implying …" said Mrs. Tickham.

109   The squirrel lowered the vacuum cleaner to the ground. He held himself very still. He considered both of them. His whiskers twitched and trembled. There were cracker crumbs on his head.

considered   If you considered something, you thought about it carefully.

110   He was a squirrel.

111   Could he be a superhero, too? Alfred T. Slipper was a janitor. Most of the time, people looked right past him. Sometimes (often, in fact) they treated him with disdain. They had no idea of the astonishing acts of heroism, the blinding light, contained within his outward, humdrum disguise.

112   Only Alfred's parakeet, Dolores, knew who he was and what he could do.

113   "The world will misunderstand him," said Flora.

114   "You bet it will," said Mrs. Tickham.

115   Mr. Tickham called out, "Are you done vacuuming? What about the Ulysses? Are you just going to leave it sitting there?"

116   "Ulysses," whispered Flora. She felt a shiver run from the back of her head to the base of her spine. She might be a natural-born cynic, but she knew the right word when she heard it.

117   "Ulysses," she said again.

118   She bent down and held out her hand to the squirrel.

119   "Come here, Ulysses," she said.

disdain   If you treat someone with disdain, you act as if he or she is unimportant or not as good as you are.

120   She spoke to him.

121   And he understood her.

122   What the girl said was, "Ulysses. Come here, Ulysses."

123   And without thinking, he moved toward her.

124   "It's okay," she said.

125   And he believed her. It was astonishing. Everything was astonishing. The setting sun was illuminating each blade of grass. It was reflecting off the girl's glasses, making a halo of light around the girl's round head, setting the whole world on fire.

126   The squirrel thought, *When did things become so beautiful? And if it has been this way all along, how is it that I never noticed before?*

127   "Listen to me," the girl said. "My name is Flora. Your name is Ulysses."

128   *Okay,* thought the squirrel.

129   She put her hand on him. She picked him up. She cradled him in her left arm.

130   He felt nothing but happiness. Why had he always been so terrified of humans? He couldn't imagine.

Collaborative Discussion

Look back on what you wrote on page 18. Tell a partner two things you learned about Flora. Then work with a group to discuss the questions below. Refer to *Flora & Ulysses* to support your ideas. Take notes for your responses. When you speak, use your notes.

1 Reread pages 24–25. What words and actions in the text show what Flora is like?

> She hates romance and she likes a comic series of a superhero

2 Review pages 36–37. How is Mrs. Tickham's reaction to what has happened to the squirrel different from Flora's?

> Mrs. TickHian had a brain Tumor

3 What words and phrases show how the squirrel is different after his experience with the vacuum cleaner?

> That he's more stonger and powerful and wasn't scared of humans anymore

Listening Tip

Listen to each speaker's ideas. How can you link them to your own ideas?

Speaking Tip

Think about how discussion ideas are related. Point out how your ideas connect to what another speaker has said.

Write a Story Scene

PROMPT

In *Flora & Ulysses,* you read about an unusual set of events that results in an equally unusual friendship between a girl and a squirrel.

Imagine that you and Flora are good friends. Use information from *Flora & Ulysses* to write a new scene from the story that tells what Flora would say to you about her friendship with Ulysses. Don't forget to use some of the Critical Vocabulary words in your writing.

PLAN

Write notes about important events that tell about Flora and Ulysses. Then write numbers next to the notes to show the order in which the events happened.

Now write your story scene in which Flora tells you about her friendship with Ulysses.

Make sure your story scene

- ☐ begins by introducing the characters.

- ☐ uses information from the text to tell about about Flora and Ulysses's friendship.

- ☐ presents events in an order that makes sense.

- ☐ uses dialogue, description, and sensory details to tell the story.

- ☐ provides a conclusion.

Prepare to Read

GENRE STUDY **Narrative poetry** tells a story using poetic structure.

- A narrative poem includes story elements such as characters and plot.

- The narrator or characters in this type of poetry reflect on a particular topic.

- Some narrative poems are written in free verse. They do not have a regular pattern of rhythm or rhyme.

SET A PURPOSE **Think about** the title of the selection. What does it make you think of? What do you hope to learn about the characters in the poetry? Write your ideas below.

CRITICAL VOCABULARY

heritage

ancient

Meet the Authors:
Alma Flor Ada (shown) and F. Isabel Campoy

YES! WE ARE LATINOS

Los Ángeles
CALIFORNIA

MEXICO

Tampa
FLORIDA

BY **ALMA FLOR ADA** AND
F. ISABEL CAMPOY

ILLUSTRATED BY **Laura Pérez**

My Name Is José Miguel— not Joe, not Mike

I am Cuban and Nicaraguan.
I live in Tampa, Florida.
I am Latino.

TAMPA, Florida

CUBA

NICARAGUA

1 **"*Adiós*, José Miguel.**
Have a good day, *hijo*.
Aprende mucho—learn all you can."
Just as he does every day,
5 my grandfather comes to the door
to say good-bye to me,
giving me advice as I leave for school.
He says he wishes he had been able
to do that for his own son, my father.
10 The sky is covered with dark clouds,
so I rush.

Grandfather

José Miguel

School is not far,
but the rain could begin any minute.
Here in Florida the sky
15 goes from blue to black in an instant
and you get soaked
before you even realize it is raining.
Roger catches up with me
before the rain does.
20 I would have rather gotten soaked.
He slaps me on the back,
pretending to be friendly
but making sure it hurts.
"Made many tacos, today,
25 Miguuuel?" he asks.

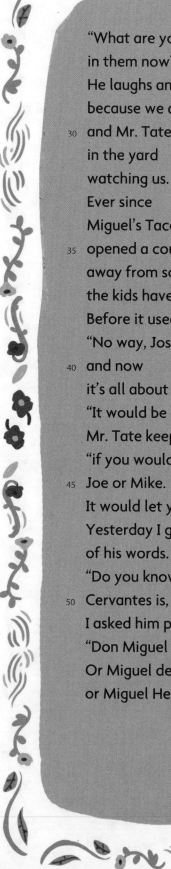

"What are you using
in them now? Dog meat?"
He laughs and lets go of me
because we are already at school,
30 and Mr. Tate is standing
in the yard
watching us.
Ever since
Miguel's Tacos
35 opened a couple of blocks
away from school,
the kids have been teasing me.
Before it used to be all about
"No way, José,"
40 and now
it's all about Miguel's Tacos.
"It would be easier,"
Mr. Tate keeps saying to me,
"if you would let us call you
45 Joe or Mike.
It would let you blend in."
Yesterday I got tired
of his words.
"Do you know who
50 Cervantes is, Mr. Tate?"
I asked him politely.
"Don Miguel de Cervantes?
Or Miguel de Unamuno,
or Miguel Hernández?

55 Look them up, Mr. Tate."
I was very sure to keep
my tone soft, my words polite.
"Google them.
Then you would know
60 why I can't be called Mike."
I think I impressed him.
I doubt he will come back
with that Mike business again.
Although the truth is that
65 I wasn't named
for Miguel de Unamuno,
or Miguel Hernández,
or Cervantes.
I was named
70 after my grandfather,
José Miguel Martínez,
who never wrote a word
but every morning
walks out to the door
75 to say good-bye
and tell me to learn much.
That is why I will not be Joe,
or Mike,
in spite of all the Rogers in the world,
80 but José Miguel Martínez.
Cubano, a mucha honra. Yes, very proud
to be Cuban.
Para servirle. And at your service.

My Name Is Lili

I am Guatemalan. I am Chinese.
I live in Los Angeles.
I am Latina.

My Name Is Michiko

I am Peruvian. I am Japanese,
a sansei.
I live in Los Angeles.
I am Latina.

CHINA

JAPAN

Los Ángeles

GUATEMALA

PERÚ

1 **I'm used to the expressions**
   of surprise and wonder
   the first time people hear me
   speaking Spanish.
5 They often make comments like,
   "For you Chinese people,
   learning languages must be easy."
   Sometimes I get tired of explaining
   that while it's true
10 I'm Chinese,
   it's also true I'm a Latina,
   a Latin American, a Guatemalan.
   It's nice when I don't have to explain.

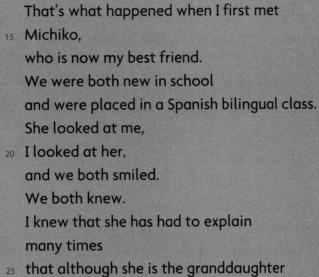

That's what happened when I first met

15 Michiko,

who is now my best friend.

We were both new in school

and were placed in a Spanish bilingual class.

She looked at me,

20 I looked at her,

and we both smiled.

We both knew.

I knew that she has had to explain

many times

25 that although she is the granddaughter

of Japanese grandparents,

Spanish is her first language.

Just as I have had to explain

that I am both Chinese and Latina.

30 It was easy to become friends,

knowing something about each other already.

We are both proud of our rich history.
I am sorry I do not speak more Chinese,
and Michiko

35 is sorry she only speaks a little Japanese.
But we are beginning to learn
our grandparents' languages.
If people continue
to think of us

40 as Chinese and Japanese,
it will be fun to at least speak
our heritage language.
In our case,
being best friends,

45 we both decided to learn
Chinese and Japanese.
We already know that two languages
are much better than one—
so imagine knowing four!

> **heritage**   A person's heritage is the beliefs and traditions passed down from the people who lived before him or her.

50 **I'm Michiko,**
and I agree
with all Lili has said.
I like the pride I feel
being from Peru—
55 a country with such extraordinary
ancient cultures—
and I feel the same pride
knowing that my grandparents' culture
is equally ancient and rich.

ancient   If something is ancient, it is very, very old.

But above all
I love talking to people,
listening to what they have to say,
trying to understand
how much people
can have inside.
That's why I will continue
to study languages,
so that one day
I can speak
and listen
around the world
and always feel at home
and among friends.

Collaborative Discussion

Look back at what you wrote on page 44. Tell a partner what you learned about the characters. Then work with a group to discuss the questions below. Refer to *Yes! We Are Latinos* to support your ideas. Take notes. When you speak, use your notes.

1 Reread the first four lines on page 46. What do you learn about José Miguel from this statement?

2 Review pages 50–52. How are Lili and Michiko the same? How are they different?

3 How do the speakers in both poems think and feel about their special heritage?

Listening Tip

Notice when a speaker uses text details to support an idea. Decide if you need to ask the speaker to explain more about the idea.

Speaking Tip

When you share an idea, point out the exact phrases or lines in the poems that led you to your conclusions.

Write a Welcome Guide

In *Yes! We Are Latinos,* you read about how three young people feel when they go to school and interact with their teachers and classmates.

Imagine that you are on your school's welcome committee. Write a welcome guide that describes ways to make new students in your school feel welcome. Use information from *Yes! We Are Latinos* and your own experiences to develop your ideas. Don't forget to use some of the Critical Vocabulary words in your writing.

PLAN

Make notes about the problems or concerns described by the characters in the text.

WRITE

Now write a welcome guide that makes new students feel welcome.

Make sure your welcome guide

- ☐ begins by introducing your topic.

- ☐ includes details from the text to support your ideas.

- ☐ is organized in a logical way, using text features to highlight key ideas.

- ☐ uses a variety of sentence types.

- ☐ ends with a concluding sentence.

Prepare to Read

GENRE STUDY **Realistic fiction** tells a story about characters and events that are like those in real life.

- Realistic fiction includes dialogue to develop the story. Dialogue is a conversation between characters.

- Realistic fiction includes a theme or lesson learned by the main character.

- Authors of realistic fiction sometimes tell the story through first-person point of view. In first-person point of view, a character in the story is the narrator.

SET A PURPOSE **Look at** the picture on page 59. Pacy, the main character, tells the story. What are some things you'd like to learn about her? Write your ideas below.

**Meet the Author:
Grace Lin**

**CRITICAL
VOCABULARY**

resolutions

doubts

relying

clumsy

awkward

The Year of the Rat

by **Grace Lin** ❀ illustrated by **Qu Lan**

1 *It's the Chinese Year of the Rat, which is believed to bring change and new beginnings, and Pacy has had more than her fair share of change. Her best friend Melody has moved to California, and her friendship with Becky and Charlotte has become strained. The new boy in school, Dun-Wei, and his family have moved into Melody's old house, making Dun-Wei "the enemy." To make matters worse, Pacy wants to be an author and illustrator when she grows up, but her father thinks that profession is a "cold door"—a difficult job that could lead to a hard life. Born in the year of the tiger, Pacy doesn't feel the luck that tigers are believed to have. Now, as the year comes to a close, Pacy thinks about the resolutions she made at the beginning of the year.*

resolutions Resolutions are promises to do or not do something.

2 The weather seemed to turn cold in a snap. Even though we thought we were ready, everyone was surprised when snow fell from the sky as if someone were pouring down sugar.

3 "Lots of snow today!" Dad said in the morning. "You lucky kids! The radio said that there's no school. It's so cold outside that it's breaking records. I wish I could have a snow day. I'm going to turn into a snowman going to work today." No school! It was like a surprise vacation. I was all ready to go outside and play until I opened the door. BRRR! The cold wind bit my face, and the inside of my nose stung as if icicles suddenly formed there. I closed the door.

4 "It's so cold out there!" I said, shivering. "It froze my nose!" Dad laughed and said, "I warned you. That's what you get when you open a cold door!"

5 All of a sudden, Dad saying that reminded me about the other cold door—the cold door of becoming an author and illustrator. Even though I didn't have any doubts about my talent anymore, I still didn't like that door. But for almost two years, I had thought that being an author and illustrator was what I wanted to be and who I was going to become. Now, I just didn't know. Was being an author and illustrator just a wishful dream, or was it something I could make happen? Was it even something I should try to make happen?

> **doubts** If you have doubts, you aren't sure about something.

6 "Remember at Chinese New Year when we wrote resolutions?" I asked Dad. "Remember how you told me some things you made happen and other things you just wished?"

7 Dad nodded.

8 "Well, how do you know which is which?" I asked. "And how do you know which are the things you should try for?"

9 "Well, this is a hard question for so early in the morning," Dad said. "Hmm, I guess it's different for every person. You have to know yourself what you can do."

10 "Can't someone just tell me?" I said. "It's too hard to figure it out."

11 "No, no one can tell you," Dad said. "Only you can decide, because only you know who you are."

12 "You know who I am," I said. "And Mom, too. You're my parents."

13 "We are your parents," Dad said. "But that doesn't mean we truly know you. It's like that little story . . ."

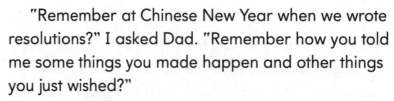

Knowing the Fish

14   One day two philosophers were walking outdoors. As they crossed a bridge, they stopped and saw an orange fish glide through the muddy green water, like floating tangerine peels. In the sunlight, the fish sparkled like fireflies.

15   "The fish are happy today," one philosopher said to the other.

16   "How do you know?" the other philosopher replied. "You're not a fish."

17   The friends continued walking. Their footsteps crunched the carpet of golden leaves as they passed, and each was quiet. The first philosopher was deep in thought, considering their conversation.

18   Finally he said to the other, "How do you know that I don't know that the fish are happy?" the first philosopher said. "You are not me."

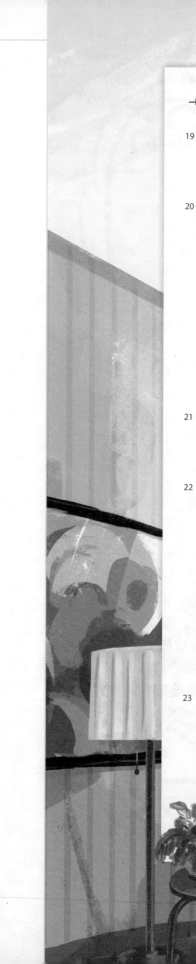

19   "So, you see," Dad said, "only you really know yourself, and only you can really make your decisions."

20   And I guessed Dad was right. It was up to me. All the things I didn't like—being scared of the cold door, feeling ashamed about Dun-Wei and being Chinese, getting bad grades, feeling weird with Becky and Charlotte, even trying to get Sam Mercer to notice me—I was the one who had to change those things. And knowing that was a little scary. "Why do you look so frightened all of a sudden?" Dad asked.

21   "I didn't realize I'd have to decide and do things," I said. "I liked it better when you and Mom did everything."

22   "Ah, you're growing up," Dad said. "Don't worry, it's not that bad. Do you remember how I told you the story about the twelve animals of Chinese New Year? The tiger came in third place, without a raft or friends helping him. He looked at the wild and fierce waters and went in, relying on just himself, his courage and strength to get across. You were born in the year of the tiger, so you're brave. You can face anything."

23   Dad's words warmed me as if I had put on a fur coat. I could be brave. I didn't need tiger luck; I was a tiger. I could almost feel the

relying   When you are relying on someone, you are trusting or depending on that person.

tiger stripes on my back. I wouldn't let the changes of the Year of the Rat sink me.

24   That night, Melody was so excited when she called me I could barely understand what she was saying.

25   "Guess what?" she said. "Guess what? I'm coming back to New Hartford to visit!"

26   I couldn't believe it, but it was true. Melody was going to come back to visit. Her parents were selling the house to Dun-Wei's family, and Melody's mom had to come back and take care of some paperwork and details. Melody's mom asked if she could stay with us while she was here, and she was going to bring Melody because "We know you two would never forgive us if I came alone."

27   But they weren't coming until around Chinese New Year. That seemed SO far away. But, luckily, the winter days were blowing by. In school we were doing open projects again, about endangered animals. And this time, I was making a book.

28   "Are you sure you don't want to be a third partner?" Becky asked out on the playground at recess. We were watching the boys play football in the snow. The boys liked to play football in the snow because then they could dive on the ground without getting hurt. We liked to watch because it was funny to see them covered in snow—especially Sam Mercer, who rolled around so much that he looked like a gingerbread cookie with white icing. "You'll have to do all that work on panda bears by yourself," Becky added.

29   "That's okay," I said. "If I want to be an author and illustrator, I better practice as much as I can."

30   "What if you don't become an author and illustrator?" Charlotte asked. "Then you would have done all that practicing for nothing."

31   "It won't be for nothing," I said, trying to feel as brave as a tiger. "I know I'm going to be one, no matter what."

32   And after I said that, I did feel like a brave tiger. What did I care about cold doors when I had fur that was thick and warm? Just like the tiger that jumped into the wild water because he wanted to win the race, I was going to jump through the door and become an author and illustrator. I wouldn't be afraid anymore.

33   "So, when is Melody coming back?" Charlotte asked. I had told them all about her phone call that morning.

34   "In a couple of months," I said, smiling. "Just in time for Chinese New Year."

35   "Well, maybe it's good you're doing the project by yourself, then," Becky said in a funny voice. "We won't see you at all once Melody arrives."

36   I stopped smiling. Suddenly I understood why everything felt clumsy and awkward when I was with Charlotte and Becky. When Melody had moved here two years ago, we had become best friends, and I had stopped being such good friends with Becky and Charlotte. Not only had I ignored them and probably hurt their feelings, all the things that I had been

> **clumsy** If an action is clumsy, it happens in a careless way.
> **awkward** In an awkward situation, things feel tense and uncomfortable.

interested in and cared about were different now. They hadn't changed. I had changed.

37   "Wow, look at that throw!" Charlotte said as a ball whizzed through the air. "Who threw that?"

38   "It was Dumb-Way!" Becky said. "Can you believe it? I guess Dumb-Way is a pretty good football player."

39   I took a deep breath and gathered my tiger strength. If I was ever going to make things better with Becky and Charlotte, I'd have let them know how I had changed. I had to let them know that the things that wouldn't have bothered me before, bothered me now.

40   "I don't think it's nice to call him Dumb-Way," I said. "His name is Dun-Wei."

41 "But everyone calls him that," Becky said.

42 I swallowed hard and looked at my feet. "I don't," I said, "because I think it's kind of mean."

43 When I peeked up, I saw Becky looking at me with her head cocked like a surprised pigeon. Slowly, she nodded. "You're right," she said. "It is mean. I won't do it anymore."

44 "Thanks," I said, and it was as if the ice in my stomach had suddenly melted away. "You know what? When Melody comes, you two should come over. I bet my mom would let me have a sleepover."

45 "Yeah, that'd be fun!" Charlotte said, and they smiled at me.

46 I smiled back. Everything would be all right. Deep inside of me, I heard a tiger roar. It was so loud and strong I was surprised. I never knew it was there before.

Collaborative Discussion

Look back at what you wrote on page 58. Tell a partner what you learned about Pacy. Then write notes about the questions below before discussing them with a group. Refer to details in *The Year of the Rat* to support your ideas.

1 Review pages 60–63. What are two kinds of cold doors in this story? Why does Pacy's dad think that becoming an author and illustrator is a cold door?

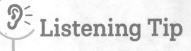

2 Reread page 66 and pages 71–72. In what ways is Pacy like a tiger?

3 What important life lessons does Pacy learn?

 Listening Tip

Concentrate on what each speaker is saying. Be ready to ask questions or add useful information.

💬 **Speaking Tip**

Read the story carefully ahead of time. Make notes about ideas you would like to share.

Write a Retelling

PROMPT ·

In *The Year of the Rat,* you read about Pacy's dream to become an author.
The story is written in first person with Pacy telling her own story.

Imagine how *The Year of the Rat* would be different if someone other than Pacy
were telling it. Pretend that you are one of the characters in *The Year of the Rat.*
Write a retelling of an event as if you were telling the story instead of Pacy.
Picture the event in your mind. How might the character's view of events be
different from Pacy's? How will it be the same? Don't forget to use some of the
Critical Vocabulary words in your writing.

PLAN ·

Summarize an event from the story that you would like to retell from a
different character's point of view.

WRITE

Now write your retelling of an event from *The Year of the Rat* from another character's point of view.

✓ Make sure your retelling

☐	retells the event using the first-person point of view.
☐	uses information from the text to retell the story.
☐	presents events in an order that makes sense.
☐	uses a variety of sentence types.
☐	provides a conclusion.

Notice & Note
Aha Moment

Prepare to Read

GENRE STUDY A **folktale** is a traditional story that has been passed down orally from one generation to another and includes the beliefs of a culture.

- Authors of folktales tell the story through the plot, or the main events of the story.

- Folktales include a lesson learned.

- Folktales might include creatures with special talents or animals that speak and have other human qualities.

SET A PURPOSE **Think about** the genre and title of this text. What questions do you have about Kitoto? Write your answer in the box below.

Written by:
Tololwa M. Mollel
Illustrated by:
Kristi Frost

CRITICAL VOCABULARY
cautiously
trickle
marveled
mighty
distant
proclaimed
majestic
sumptuous
hoard

KITOTO THE MIGHTY

BY **TOLOLWA M. MOLLEL**

ILLUSTRATED BY **KRISTI FROST**

1. **H**igh in the sky, a hawk circled and searched. Then, swift as an arrow, he dropped to the ground.

2. Barely ahead of the hawk's claws, Kitoto darted into a bush. The little mouse who had never learned to dig burrows hid there, with nothing to eat all day.

3. The next morning, before the sun was up or the hawk awoke, Kitoto scurried hungrily across the Savannah. He found a fallen baobab fruit. But another creature had seen it first, and the delicious seeds were gone.

4   That is when the hungry little mouse heard the sound of a big, rushing river. Cautiously, he approached the riverbank and watched the angry water sweep away huge trees and rocks.

5   "How powerful the river is!" thought Kitoto. And he had an idea.

6   "I am Kitoto the Mouse, small and weak," he cried to the river. "I wish to make friends with you. With a friend like you to protect me, I won't have to go hungry for fear of the hawk. You must be the most powerful of all beings."

7   "Not so," roared the river. "The sun can protect you better for he is far more powerful than I. He burns me to a trickle in the dry season. The sun is the most powerful being."

> **cautiously**   If you do something cautiously, you do it very carefully.
> **trickle**   A trickle is a small amount of slowly flowing water.

8   The river wove a beautiful nest of steam, placed Kitoto inside, and gently blew it above the trees and mountains, into the soft sunlight.

9   "Why, I am bigger than the Savannah!" Kitoto marveled, as the earth below grew smaller and smaller. He felt very pleased with himself. Still, he had never in his life imagined making friends with one as powerful as the sun.

10   "I must do my best to impress him," Kitoto decided, as he arrived at the sun's home late in the day.

11   Sparks swirled as the weary sun stoked and fanned his dying log fire.

12   Kitoto puffed himself up importantly. "I am Kitoto the Mighty, Master of the Savannah," he announced. "I wish to make friends with the most powerful being. I thought it was the river. But no, the river tells me it is you."

13   The sun, wrapped in a blanket, shivered in the chill of dusk. "Not so," he replied. "There is one far more powerful than I, who gathers the clouds and hides the Savannah from my view. The wind is the most powerful being."

---

marveled   If you marveled at something, you felt surprised or amazed by it.
mighty   Something that is mighty is strong and powerful.

14   In the morning, the sun sent Kitoto across the heavens on a beam from a fresh log fire. Kitoto peered at the Savannah, small as a nut, far, far below, and felt very grand indeed.

15   He found the wind hard at work, tugging the clouds together. "I am Kitoto the Great, King of the Savannah," he declared. "I wish to make friends with the most powerful being. I thought it was the river, who told me it was the sun. But no, the sun tells me it is you."

16   "Not so," replied the wind. "There is one far more powerful than I, one I cannot tug with my strong braids, however hard I try. The mountain is the most powerful being."

17   With the longest of her braids, the wind swung Kitoto away to a distant mountain peak.

18   "I am Kitoto the Magnificent, Emperor of the Savannah," the little mouse proclaimed to the mountain. "I wish to make friends with the most powerful being. I thought it was the river, who told me it was the sun, who told me it was the wind. But no, the wind tells me it is you."

19   "Not so," thundered the majestic mountain. "There is one far more powerful than I, who chomps away at my root. Surely this creature, whom I have felt but never seen, must be the most powerful being of all."

---

distant   If something is distant, it is far away.

proclaimed   If you proclaimed something, you said it in a strong way to show it was important for others to hear.

majestic   Something that is majestic is impressive and beautiful.

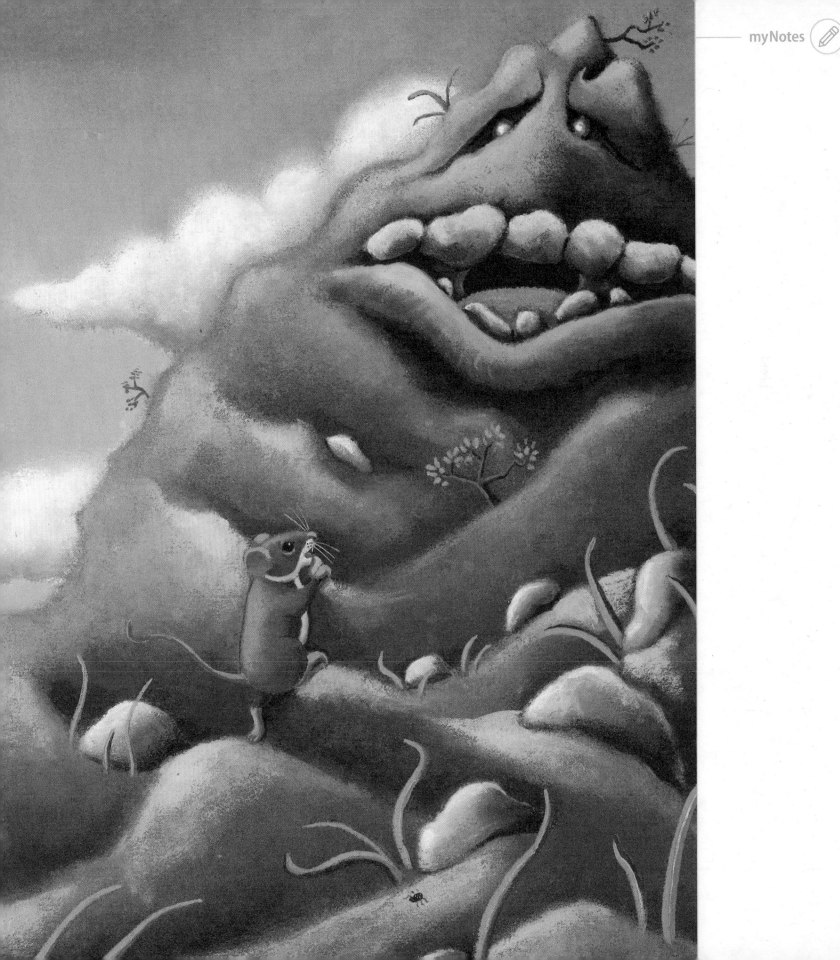

20   Then the mountain rumbled and opened wide, allowing Kitoto to enter.

21   Down, down Kitoto scampered, through dark pathways, deep to the root of the mountain. There, he found himself in a huge maze of tunnels, archways, halls, and chambers. The walls were cool and smooth and smelled pleasantly. Tiny, shiny pebbles lit the way.

22   At every bend, Kitoto expected to see a giant loom before him, for a giant it must be, he thought, to carve such a world out of the mountain.

23   A sound from the shadows startled him. In his fear, Kitoto forgot to be Mighty or Great, Master, King or Emperor. "Please do not harm me," he pleaded with the unseen giant. "It is only Kitoto the Mouse, small and weak. I wish to make friends with you, the most powerful of all beings. With you to protect me I won't have to go hungry for fear of the hawk." Kitoto waited, trembling.

24   From the shadows, a figure stepped forward.

25   Kitoto stared in amazement as the figure bowed.

26   "I am Kigego, the mountain mouse. Welcome to my home."

27   "*Your* home? *You* built all this?" Kitoto asked. "The paths, the tunnels . . . *everything?*"

28   "Everything," replied Kigego. "With nothing more than my teeth and a lot of hard work." Her eyes glowed proudly. "Come."

29   Like old friends, the two mice explored the winding pathways.

30   They enjoyed a game of hide and seek in the mazes.

31   They played catch with shiny pebbles.

32   Then they fell asleep on cushions of soft earth.

33   When they awoke, Kigego unearthed a sumptuous hoard of bulbs, tubers, and roots. "I'll teach you the secrets of the ground," she promised, chuckling.

34   Kitoto chuckled back and said, "And I will teach you the secrets of the Savannah."

sumptuous   Something that is sumptuous is impressive and expensive-looking.

hoard   A hoard is a group of valuable things that is usually kept secret and carefully guarded by someone.

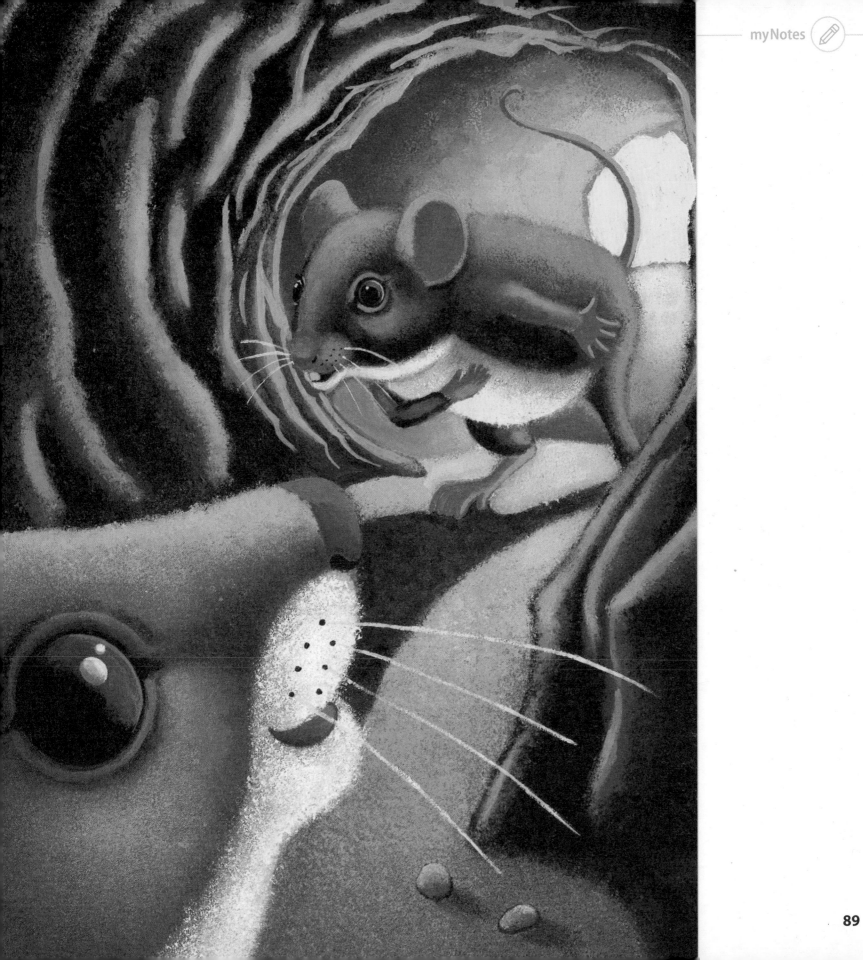

35   High in the sky, a hawk circled and searched. Deep at the root
of a mountain, two friends chewed merrily away. And after the
hawk had gone to sleep, they ventured out to enjoy the sweet, cool
night air.

36   To this very day, few would guess that the mouse is the most
powerful being on the big, wide Savannah. But the rushing river, the
weary sun, the tugging wind—even the majestic mountain, will tell
you this is so.

Collaborative Discussion

Look back on what you wrote on page 76. Tell a partner something you learned about Kitoto. Make notes about the questions below. Then work with a group to discuss the questions. Refer to details in *Kitoto the Mighty* to support your ideas.

1 Reread pages 78–79. Why does Kitoto seek out the most powerful being?

2 Review pages 80–85. What words does Kitoto use to describe himself when he meets the sun, the wind, and the mountain? What do you learn about him from these words?

3 What do you think Kitoto learns about himself when he meets the powerful being in the mountain? How do you know?

Listening Tip

Listen carefully to what others say. Wait until a speaker has finished before adding your ideas.

Speaking Tip

State your ideas in a voice that is loud enough for everyone to hear, but be careful not to yell.

Write a Journal Entry

PROMPT ....

In *Kitoto the Mighty,* you read about a mouse who searches for the most powerful creature and learns about the power that he has, too. The story describes the events in sequential order.

Imagine that you are one of the characters that Kitoto meets. Use details from *Kitoto the Mighty* to write a journal entry about the day you met Kitoto. Don't forget to use some of the Critical Vocabulary words in your writing.

PLAN ....

Summarize the event from the story in which Kitoto meets the character you've selected. Make notes about the character and key details about the event.

WRITE

Now write your journal entry about the day you met Kitoto.

KITOTO
THE
MIGHTY

BY TOLOLWA M. MOLLEL
ILLUSTRATED BY KRISTI FROST

✓

Make sure your journal entry
☐ begins by introducing the characters and setting.
☐ uses first-person pronouns such as *I, me,* and *my.*
☐ uses information from the text to describe the thoughts and feelings of the chosen character.
☐ describes events in an order that makes sense.
☐ provides a conclusion.

? Essential Question

How do your experiences help shape your identity?

Write a Story

PROMPT Think about the stories you read in this module.

Imagine that your class is writing a book of superhero adventures for the class library. Write a story that tells how Ulysses and Kitoto work together to solve a problem. Be sure to include details from *Flora & Ulysses* and *Kitoto the Mighty*.

I will write a story about _____.

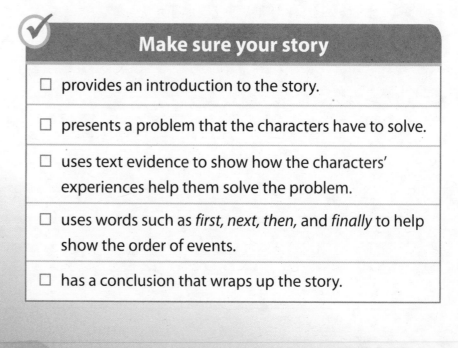

✓ Make sure your story

- ☐ provides an introduction to the story.

- ☐ presents a problem that the characters have to solve.

- ☐ uses text evidence to show how the characters' experiences help them solve the problem.

- ☐ uses words such as *first, next, then,* and *finally* to help show the order of events.

- ☐ has a conclusion that wraps up the story.

What details from the selections will help you describe the superheroes' adventure? Look back at your notes and revisit *Flora & Ulysses* and *Kitoto the Mighty* to look for details about the characters that show how they are like superheroes.

Write details that tell about each character in the word web below.

My Topic: _____

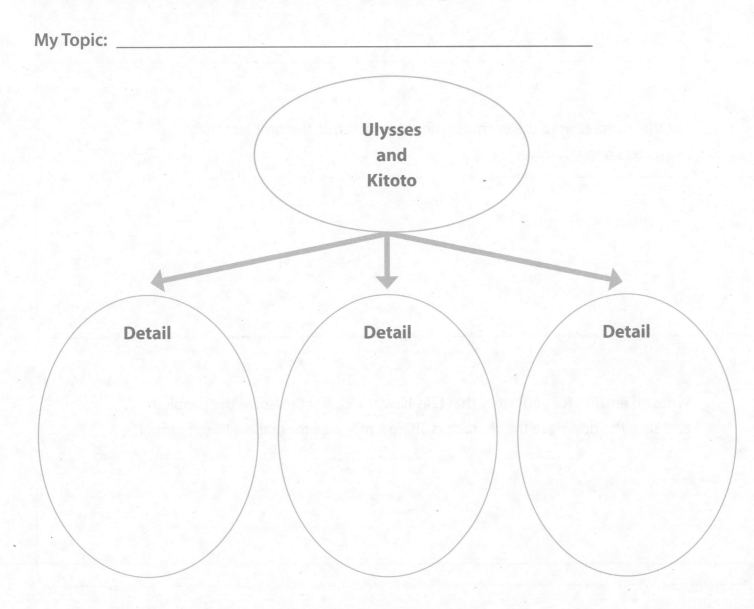

Ulysses
and
Kitoto

Detail

Detail

Detail

DRAFT .... Write your story.

Use your web to write a strong **beginning** that describes the setting and characters.

For the **middle,** write the events in the story. Describe the problem the characters need to solve.

Write an **ending** for your story that tells how the characters solve the problem and save the day. Have the characters share a message for readers to remember.

REVISE AND EDIT

Review your draft.

The revision and editing steps give you a chance to look carefully at your writing and make it even better. Work with a partner to determine whether your characters are clearly described or if there are parts of the story that you could make more exciting. Use these questions to help you evaluate and improve your story.

PURPOSE/ FOCUS	ORGANIZATION	EVIDENCE	LANGUAGE/ VOCABULARY	CONVENTIONS
☐ Is my story entertaining for readers? ☐ Have I shown how the characters work together to solve a problem?	☐ Does my story have a clear beginning, middle, and end? ☐ Have I provided a strong conclusion?	☐ Did I use text evidence to describe the characters? ☐ Did I show how their experiences helped them solve the problem?	☐ Did I use words such as *first, next, then,* and *finally* to show the order of events?	☐ Have I used correct spelling? ☐ Did I indent each new paragraph? ☐ Did I use a variety of sentence types?

PUBLISH

Share your work.

Create a Finished Copy Make a final copy of your story. You may want to include illustrations or present it in a graphic novel format. Consider these options to share your story:

 1 Publish your story on a school or class website.

 2 Add your story to an "Adventures of Ulysses and Kitoto" station in the classroom.

 3 Work with other students to present the story to the class as a readers' theater.

Come To Your Senses

"All our knowledge begins with the senses."

—Immanuel Kant

How do people and animals use their senses to navigate the world?

Get Curious

Video

Words About the Senses

The words in the chart will help you talk and write about the selections in this module. Which words about the senses have you seen before? Which words are new to you?

Add to the Vocabulary Network on page 101 by writing synonyms, antonyms, and related words and phrases for each word about the senses.

After you read each selection in this module, come back to the Vocabulary Network and keep building it. Add more ovals if you need to.

WORD	MEANING	CONTEXT SENTENCE
perception (noun)	Your perception of something is how you notice or experience it using your senses.	The amount of light in a room affects our perception of the objects in it.
aroma (noun)	An aroma is a strong, pleasant smell.	The aroma of freshly-baked cookies filled the kitchen.
distinguish (verb)	If you notice how things are different, you can distinguish them from one another.	I can distinguish the two puppies from one another because only one has a white spot on his chest.
tactile (adjective)	Something that is tactile is experienced through the sense of touch.	Petting a dog is a tactile experience.

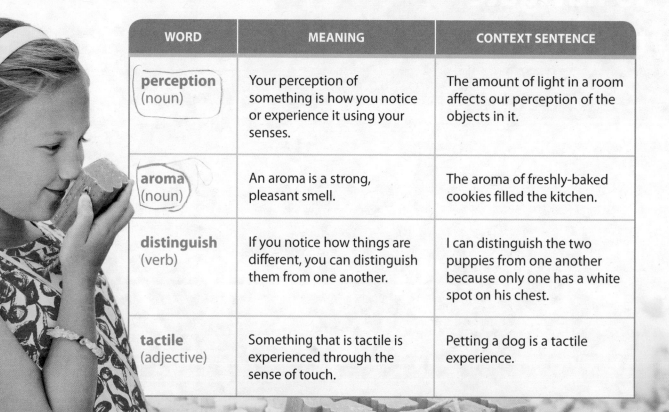

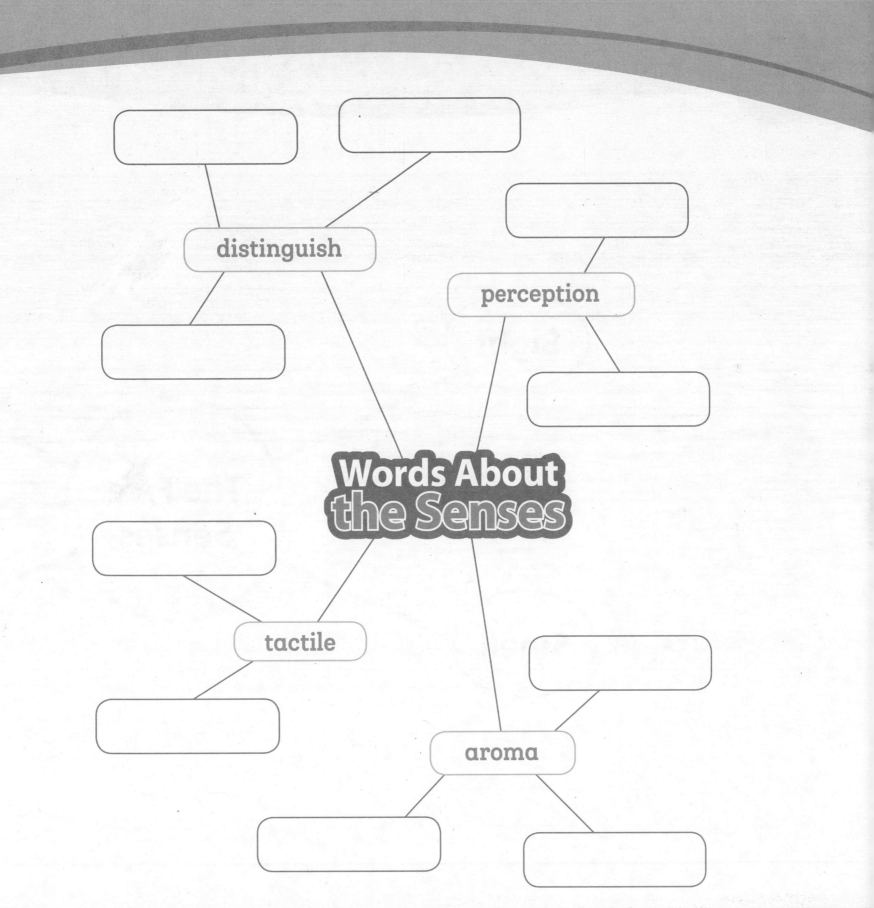

distinguish

perception

Words About the Senses

tactile

aroma

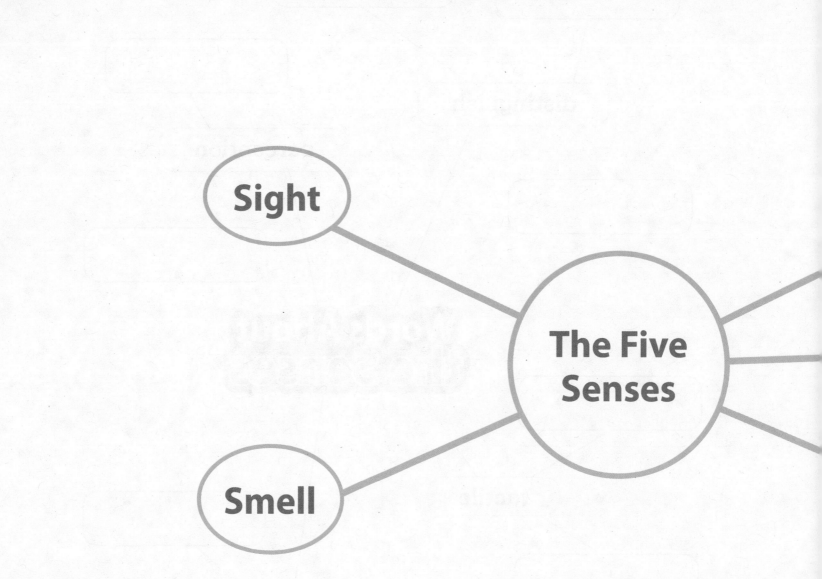

Sight

The Five Senses

Smell

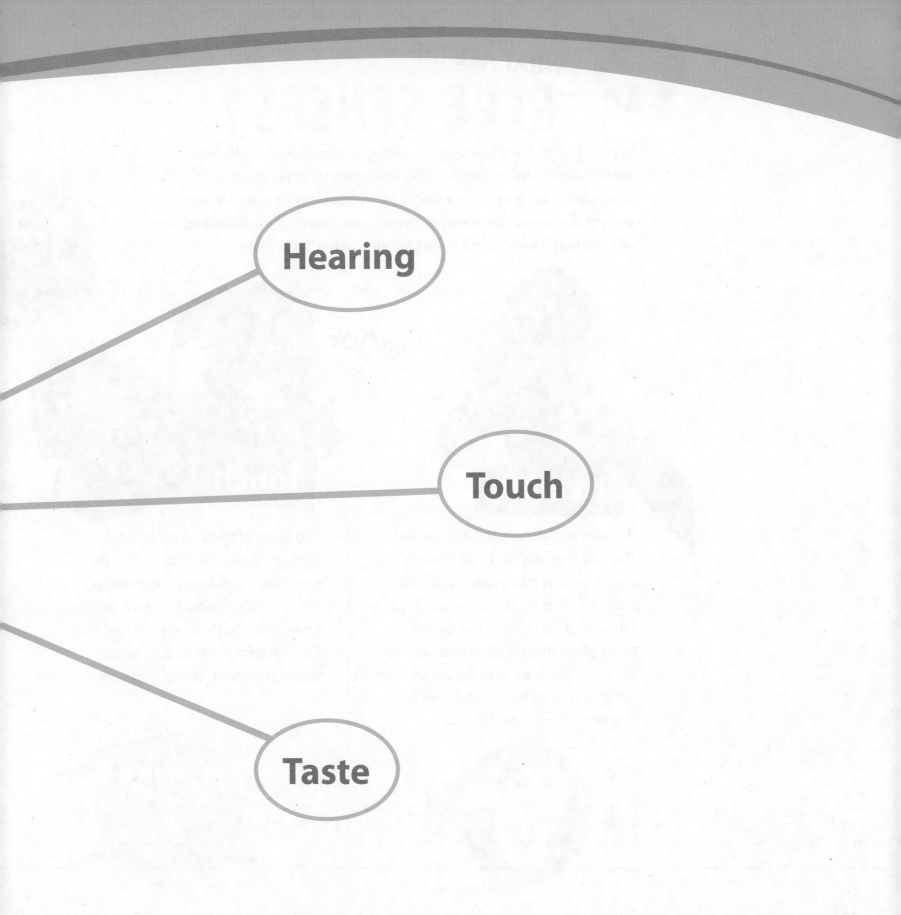

Hearing

Touch

Taste

Short Read

WHAT ARE THE
FIVE SENSES?

1 Human beings have five senses—sight, hearing, taste, smell, and touch—that help us form a perception of our surroundings. Our senses allow us to enjoy our world, learn more about it, and even protect ourselves. When we see, hear, taste, smell, or touch something, information travels to our brains to tell us what's going on.

WOOF
WOOF

Hearing

Touch

2 We have an outer ear and an inner ear. The outer ear acts like a cup to catch sounds as they move past us. Sounds enter the inner ear through a spiral-shaped tube called the *cochlea*. The auditory nerve sends the sounds as information to the brain. The brain uses this information to tell us how far away sounds are and where they're coming from.

3 The sense of touch is experienced through the whole body. When we come into contact with something, nerve endings in our skin send tactile information to the brain. We can detect four different sensations through touch: cold, heat, contact, and pain.

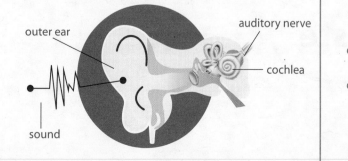

outer ear
auditory nerve
cochlea
sound

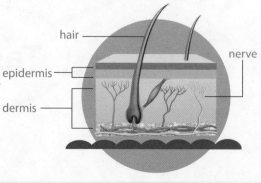

hair
nerve
epidermis
dermis

Smell

Sight

Taste

4   The olfactory nerve in the nose delivers messages about smells, or aromas, to the brain. We can detect and distinguish among seven different aromas: camphor, musk, flower, mint, ether, acrid, and putrid.

5   Our eyeballs have a lens at the front and a retina at the back. The lens focuses images onto the retina. The optic nerve sends those images as pieces of information to the brain. The brain creates a three-dimensional image that helps us tell how close we are to objects around us.

6   Our tongues are covered with tiny bumps called *taste buds*, or *papillae* (puh-pih-lee). When we taste something, the papillae send information to the brain to identify the flavor. Taste buds detect four different flavors: sweet, salty, sour, and bitter. Everything you taste includes one or more of these flavors.

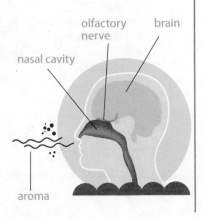

olfactory nerve | brain

nasal cavity

aroma

retina

lens

optic nerve

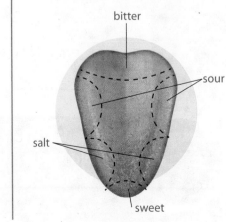

bitter

sour

salt

sweet

Prepare to Read

GENRE STUDY **Informational texts** give facts and examples about a topic.

- Authors of informational texts often organize their ideas using headings and subheadings to tell readers what each section of text is about.
- Science texts include specific words about the topic.
- Informational texts often include visuals, such as charts, diagrams, graphs, and maps.

SET A PURPOSE **Think about** the title and genre of this text. What do you know about the sense of sight? What do you want to learn? Write your ideas below.

CRITICAL VOCABULARY

luminous

transparent

reflect

illuminates

judge

**Build Background:
The Sense of Sight**

THE SCIENCE BEHIND SIGHT

BY LOUISE SPILSBURY

SEEING THINGS

1   Think about how you are reading the words on this page. You can read these words because your eyes can see. Seeing things helps us find out about the world around us.

The Sense of Sight

2   We have five senses to help us understand our world—sight, smell, touch, hearing, and taste. Sight is very important. It shows us sizes, shapes, and colors. It tells us where we are going and how far away things are. It helps us read, play, learn, watch things, and more.

Light and Dark

3   We can see when it is light, but it is hard to see well in the dark. When we go into a room with no lights or windows, it is dark. The room and the things in it look black because there is no light to help us see them.

Light gives us sight! We can see the trees in this forest because of the sunlight shining on them. ▶

LIGHT & SIGHT

4 When it is dark at bedtime and you want to read, you turn your lamp on. We use light from lamps to see when it is dark.

Luminous Things

5 Things that give off light are luminous. The sun is luminous. We use light from the sun to see things during the day. Lamps, fires, televisions, and flashlights are luminous, too.

Making Shadows

6 Light from luminous objects travels in straight lines. It can move through clear things such as air, water, and glass. That is how windows let light inside our homes so we can see. We say clear things are transparent. If you close your curtains, you stop light from getting inside. The curtains are opaque (o-pake). Opaque things do not let light through.

When light cannot pass through something, it can create a shadow. ▶

luminous   If something is luminous, it gives off light.

transparent   If an object is transparent, you can see through it.

We see things when they give off light or when light bounces off them.

Reflecting Light

7   We see luminous objects because they give off light. However, most things we see are not luminous. Tables, chairs, soccer balls, and fields do not give off light. Instead, they reflect it! Light bounces off surfaces and objects around us, and we see them when some of that reflected light enters our eyes.

More Light, More Sight

8   We can see better when it is lighter. When you are in a dark room, a candle illuminates only a small area, but if you turn on a ceiling light, it lights up the whole room. Some surfaces reflect light better than others. Black fabric does not reflect light well. Light reflects best off shiny surfaces, such as mirrors.

reflect   When light reflects off a surface, it bounces back without passing through the surface.

illuminates   Something that illuminates gives off light and makes the area around it brighter.

A candle only lights a small space. If you want more light, you have to light more candles.

HOW EYES WORK

9　An eye is shaped like a round ball. Most of it is inside your head. Do you know what the outer parts of the eye—the parts that you can see—do?

Eye Care

10　Eyelids can close quickly to protect your eyes. When an eyelid blinks, it washes the surface of the eye with tears. Tears wash dust and other things off the eye. Tears leave your eye through a tiny tube called a **tear duct**.

Letting in Light

11　The colored part of your eye is the **iris**. The black spot in the middle of the iris is an opening called the **pupil**. The pupil lets light into the eye. In bright light your eye needs to take in less light, so the pupil becomes smaller. In low light, the pupil becomes bigger, to take in more light.

12　Look at your eyes in a mirror and then close them. Open them quickly to see your pupils get smaller in bright light.

▼ These are the outer parts of the eye.

eyelid
pupil
iris
tear duct

113

Light and Lenses

13 Light passes into the eye through a lens. A lens works a bit like a magnifying glass. When you look through a magnifying glass, it makes things very clear.

14 In the same way, the lens focuses light so the image that we see is clear. It focuses the image onto the retina. The retina is the surface at the back of the eyeball. The image that the lens sends to the retina is upside down. The brain turns it the right way up, so we know what we are looking at!

▼ Light from an object passes through the lens of the eye and is focused on the retina.

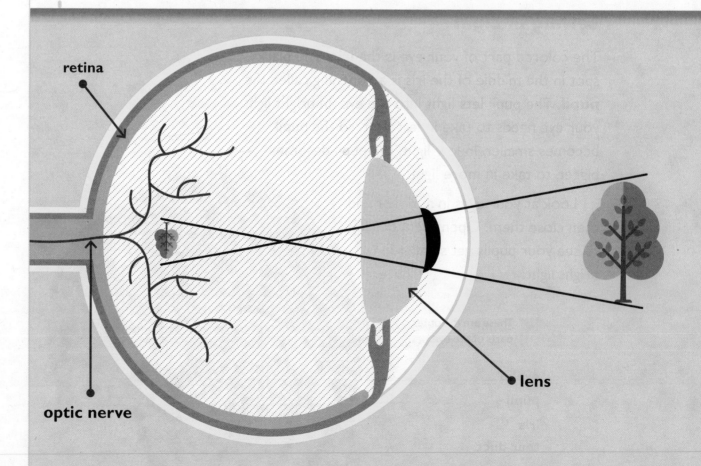

retina

optic nerve

lens

114

Messages to the Brain

15   The retina sends messages about what your eyes see to your brain. First, it changes the colors and shapes in the image into millions of signals. Then, it sends these signals to the brain along a pathway called the optic nerve. The brain figures out what the signals mean.

Lens and Distance

16   Look away from this book and focus on something far away. You will not feel it, but the shape of your lenses changes. The lens becomes thinner when the eye looks at things close-up, and it becomes thicker when the eye looks at things far away.

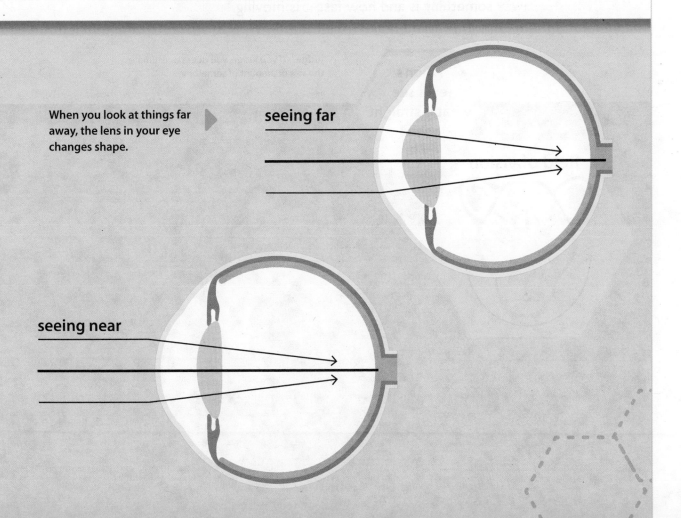

When you look at things far away, the lens in your eye changes shape.

seeing far

seeing near

ANIMAL SIGHT

17 Some animals see the world in a different way than we do. Our eyes are on the front of our heads. Rabbits and horses have eyes on the sides of their heads. What is the difference?

Eyes at the Front

18 Close one eye and try to touch the ends of two pencils together. Why is it so hard? With only one eye, you cannot judge exactly how far away things are. With two eyes at the front, each eye sees a slightly different view. The brain compares the two views to figure out exactly how far away something is and how fast it is moving.

judge If you judge, you guess or estimate the size or amount of something.

A lion's eyes see what is straight ahead of it.

field of vision

19   Foxes, lions, and most other predators (animals that hunt other animals) have two eyes on the front of their head, like us. This helps them to hunt and catch animals.

20   You cannot judge distance very well with just one eye. Try playing with a ball with one eye shut. You will find that you are more likely to get hit by the ball than catch it! Be careful not to hurt yourself!

Eyes at the Side

21   Animals with one eye on each side of their head can see when a predator comes up behind them. The downside is that the two eyes work separately. Because the images that the eyes see are so different, the brain cannot compare them to figure out exactly how far away things are.

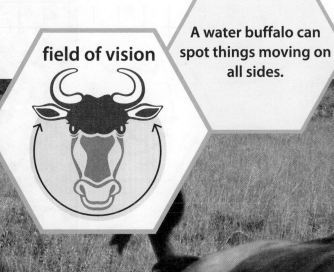

field of vision

A water buffalo can spot things moving on all sides.

Seeing at Night

22 A cat's eyes glow in the dark because they have a part behind their retinas that works a bit like a mirror. It reflects light back onto the retina. Because more light is reflected onto the retina, the cat can see more. That is why cats and some other animals can see better in low light than we can.

Pupil Power

23 To let more light into your room, you open the curtains wide. When it is nearly dark, cats' pupils open very wide to let as much light in as possible. In bright light, their pupils are very narrow. This stops their retinas from being hurt by too much light.

Can you tell which of these cats is looking into bright light and which is looking into low light?

Have you ever wondered why a cat's eyes glow in the dark?

WEARING GLASSES

24 Some people wear glasses to help them see clearly. People who are nearsighted can see things that are close clearly, but things farther away look blurry. People who are farsighted can see things that are far away clearly, but things up close look blurry. Wearing glasses helps these people to see better.

Refraction

25 Put a straw in a glass of water and look at it from the side. At certain angles, the straw looks broken. That is because the water in the glass bends light as you are looking at it. Bending light is called **refraction**.

Why Do People Need Glasses?

26 The lens in your eye refracts light to focus in on the retina. Sight problems happen when a person's lens does not refract light onto the retina properly.

How Do Glasses Work?

27 Glasses and contact lenses work by refraction. Lenses in glasses are made from pieces of transparent plastic or glass. The pieces are curved so that the lenses can bend light. Lenses bend light to focus it on the right spot on the retina. This allows the wearer to see clearly.

Glasses help some people to see better.

Nearsighted

With nearsightedness, the lens focuses the image in front of the retina.

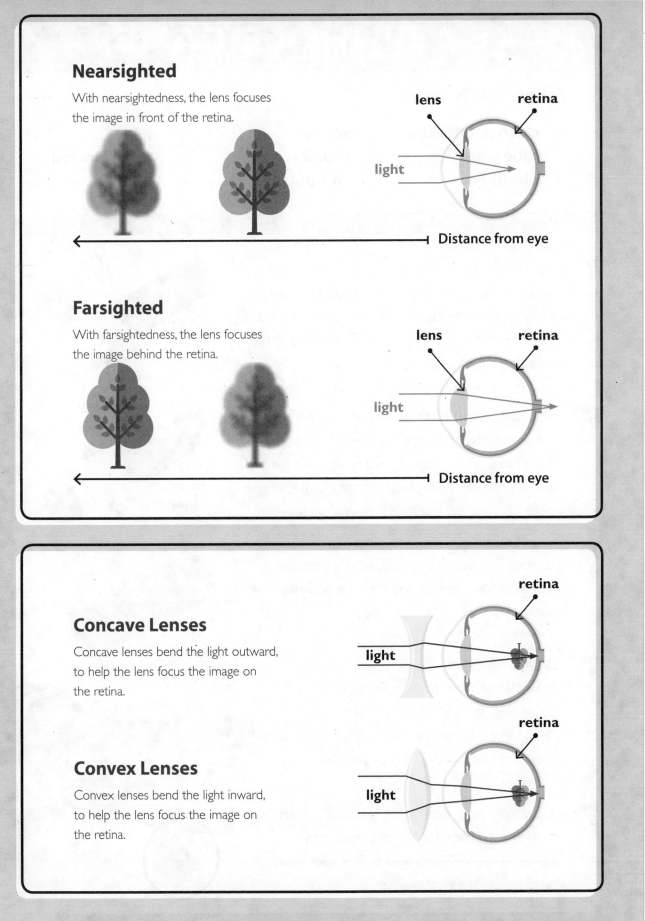

lens　　**retina**

light

Distance from eye

Farsighted

With farsightedness, the lens focuses the image behind the retina.

lens　　**retina**

light

Distance from eye

Concave Lenses

Concave lenses bend the light outward, to help the lens focus the image on the retina.

retina

light

Convex Lenses

Convex lenses bend the light inward, to help the lens focus the image on the retina.

retina

light

MAKE A PINHOLE CAMERA

What You Need:

- ☐ clean potato chip tube with a plastic lid
- ☐ scissors
- ☐ thumbtack
- ☐ wax paper
- ☐ tape
- ☐ aluminum foil

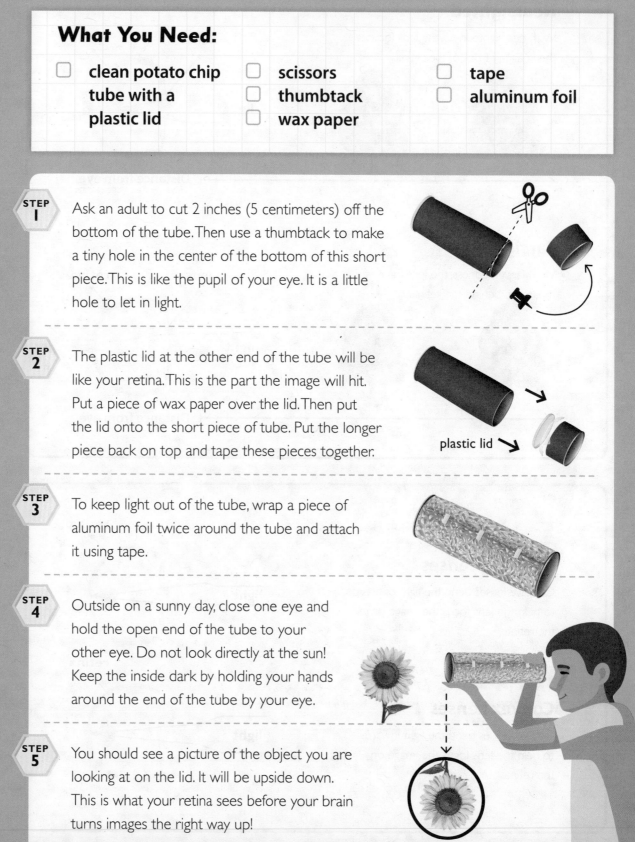

STEP 1

Ask an adult to cut 2 inches (5 centimeters) off the bottom of the tube. Then use a thumbtack to make a tiny hole in the center of the bottom of this short piece. This is like the pupil of your eye. It is a little hole to let in light.

STEP 2

The plastic lid at the other end of the tube will be like your retina. This is the part the image will hit. Put a piece of wax paper over the lid. Then put the lid onto the short piece of tube. Put the longer piece back on top and tape these pieces together.

plastic lid

STEP 3

To keep light out of the tube, wrap a piece of aluminum foil twice around the tube and attach it using tape.

STEP 4

Outside on a sunny day, close one eye and hold the open end of the tube to your other eye. Do not look directly at the sun! Keep the inside dark by holding your hands around the end of the tube by your eye.

STEP 5

You should see a picture of the object you are looking at on the lid. It will be upside down. This is what your retina sees before your brain turns images the right way up!

Collaborative Discussion

THE SCIENCE BEHIND
SIGHT
BY LOUISE SPILSBURY

Look back at what you wrote on page 106. Tell a partner two things you learned from this text. Then work with a group to discuss the questions below. Refer to details and examples in *The Science Behind Sight* to explain your answers. Take notes for your responses. When you speak, use your notes.

1 Review pages 116–117. If you closed one eye, would it be easier to put the pieces of a puzzle together? Why or why not?

2 Reread page 113. How would your eyes react if you walked outside on a sunny day?

3 Why would there be a lot of shadows in a thick forest?

Listening Tip

Listen for the specific details the speaker uses to answer a question. What details or examples can you add?

Speaking Tip

Build your ideas onto what speakers have said before you. If you agree with what a speaker has said, say so, and then add your ideas.

Write a Summary

In *The Science Behind Sight*, you read about how eyes work so that people and animals can see. The text contains diagrams that add to the information in the text.

Imagine that your class has a science blog where you share new science concepts your class has read about. It is your turn to post an update to the science blog. Write a summary of *The Science Behind Sight* to explain how light is important for the sense of sight. Don't forget to use some of the Critical Vocabulary words in your writing.

PLAN

Make notes about the main ideas and important details about light and sight you find in the text and diagrams.

Now write your summary of the information about light and sight from
The Science Behind Sight.

✓	Make sure your summary
☐	begins by introducing your topic.
☐	has a structure that clearly explains the ideas.
☐	connects ideas using words such as *then, because,* and *so.*
☐	ends with a concluding sentence.
☐	uses transition words to connect ideas.

Prepare to View

GENRE STUDY ▶ **Informational videos** present facts and information about a topic in visual and audio form.

- A narrator explains what is happening on the screen.

- Real people, places, and animals may be used to help viewers understand the topic.

- Informational videos include words that may be specific to a science or social studies topic.

- Producers of videos may include sound effects or background music to make the video more interesting for viewers.

SET A PURPOSE ▶ **As you watch,** think about the narrator's main points to help you understand how different animals use their five senses. Write your ideas below.

Build Background:
Animal Survival

CRITICAL VOCABULARY

relish

familiar

savor

enhance

ANIMAL SENSES

from *Animal Atlas*

As you watch *Animal Senses,* think about the narrator's main purpose. How does the narrator introduce new information? How is that information supported through the visuals? Does the narrator help to make the topic interesting? Why or why not? Take notes in the space below.

Listen for the Critical Vocabulary words *relish*, *familiar*, *savor*, and *enhance* for clues to the meaning of each word. Take notes in the space below about how the words were used.

relish   If you relish something, you enjoy it very much.

familiar   Something familiar is something that you know and are used to.

savor   If you savor something, you take your time enjoying it.

enhance   If you enhance something, you've made it into something better or improved upon it.

ANIMAL SENSES
from Animal Atlas

Collaborative Discussion

Look back at what you wrote on page 126. Tell a partner two things you learned about animal senses. Then work with a group to discuss the questions below. Refer to details and examples in *Animal Senses* to support your ideas. Take notes for your responses. When you speak, use your notes.

1 How do animals use their senses?

2 What does the narrator mean by "nature is the great compensator"?

3 What can you learn about an animal's life from observing where its eyes are placed?

Listening Tip

Look at the facial expressions and gestures the speaker uses to explain his or her points.

Speaking Tip

Look at the audience to make sure they understand your ideas.

Write a Description

In *Animal Senses*, you saw and heard interesting information about animals, such as how they use their sense of sight to catch food and to avoid being prey for another animal.

Now imagine that *Animal Senses* will be shown on a television station. Your job is to describe it in a guide for viewers so they will choose to watch it. Use some of the Critical Vocabulary words in your description.

Make notes about the central ideas and important details you saw and heard about animal senses. Make sure to include the most interesting information you learned.

WRITE

Now write your television guide description of *Animal Senses* in the space below.

✓	Make sure your description
☐	begins by naming the video.
☐	is organized to clearly explain your ideas.
☐	describes the main points of the video.
☐	tells why viewers should watch the video.
☐	ends with a concluding sentence.

Prepare to Read

GENRE STUDY **Personal narratives** tell about important events in a real person's life.

- Authors of personal narratives often present events in sequential, or chronological, order. This helps readers understand what happened in his or her life and when.

- Personal narratives include first-person pronouns, such as *I*, *me*, *my*, *mine*, and *we*.

- Authors of personal narratives may use humor to illustrate a point or to engage readers.

SET A PURPOSE **Look at** the photograph on the next page. The author of this personal narrative is blind. What are some things you'd like to know about him? Write your ideas below.

Build Background: Adaptations All Around

CRITICAL VOCABULARY

accepted

obstacles

command

denying

adapt

comfort

BLIND AMBITION

by Matthew Cooper ❖ as told to Rachel Buchholz

photographs by Karine Aigner

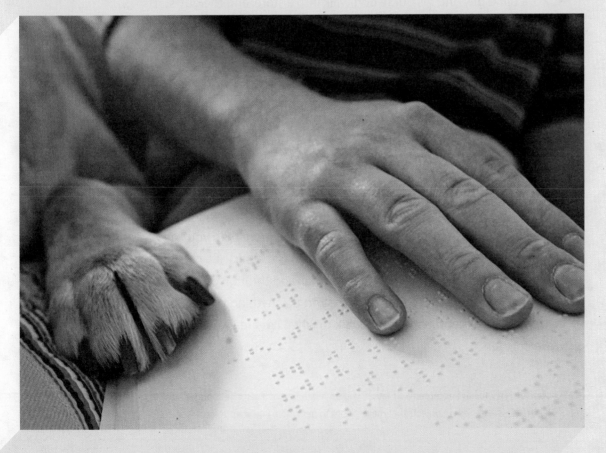

Twyla helps me fit in at school.

1   So, a blind guy and his guide dog walk into a store, and the guy starts swinging the dog around his head. The cashier goes, "Um, can I help you?" And the blind guy says, "Nah, I'm just looking around."

2   When I tell that joke, sometimes people are a little shocked. I think maybe they think that a blind person like me shouldn't be telling jokes like that. But I'll tell you what: If you can't laugh at yourself, if you can't show that you've accepted what you've been given, then there's no way you can live your life.

3   Now of course I would never swing my guide dog, Twyla, around my head. I mean, that's just a joke, especially since guide dogs really don't "see" for their owners like that. But Twyla does help me more than you can imagine. She helps me cross the street and yanks me back if a car is coming. She gets me around obstacles in the sidewalk and through crowded school hallways. She allows me to go anywhere and do anything I want. She's my companion, my friend, someone to talk to when I get really fed up. Basically, we're partners.

---

accepted   If you have accepted a situation, you understand that it can't be changed.
obstacles   Obstacles are objects that make it hard to get where you want to go.

MY PERSONAL SUPERHERO

4   I don't remember a time when I could see. When I was three I was diagnosed with a brain tumor that pressed against my optic nerve, and I gradually lost my sight. At first I walked with a cane, but canes can be awkward. I got my first guide dog when I was 11, and about a year and a half ago, I got Twyla.

5   A lot of people think that when Twyla sees a green light, she knows that it's time to cross the street. But that's not how it works. It's all on my command. So when we get to a street corner, I have to listen for cars, then *tell* her to cross the street. Or if there's a bike in the sidewalk, it's not the dog's job to move it. Her job is to figure out a way *around* the bike.

6   Is it nerve-racking to walk down a sidewalk and wonder if I'm going to fall into a big hole? Not at all. I have to trust the dog. If you start denying what the dog is telling you, she's going to get nervous and lose all her training. I *have* to trust her.

7   Twyla and I are a team. She knows my schedule at school and just takes me to class. If I need to go someplace she's not expecting, I give her directions. The idea is that if I've said, "Right," and we're not quite to the hallway, she thinks, "OK, I'll turn right at the hallway that's coming up," instead of running me into some lockers.

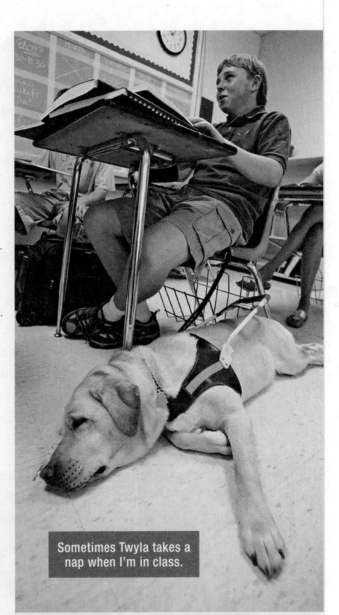

Sometimes Twyla takes a nap when I'm in class.

command   If you do something on command, you do it because you were told to.

denying   Denying something means not believing that it's true.

135

8 Twyla does have her moments. Sometimes she snores in class, which cracks everyone up. (Although once a teacher thought it was a student!) And one time some cleaning solution made the classroom floor a little slick, and Twyla hit it like Bambi on the ice, sliding all over. She still tiptoes in that classroom.

ON MY OWN

9 Twyla can't do everything for me. And it's important that I fit in with everybody, to not be known as "that blind kid." I am Matthew Cooper. That is who I am. To fit in, I know that I have to adapt.

10 So if I want to play paintball with my friends, I make them wear buzzers so I know where they are. When I wanted to run the sound system for my school plays, I put Braille labels on all the controls. (I read in Braille, which is a combination of raised dots that represent letters.)

11 My favorite thing to do is play golf. The idea is that my coach or my dad will position my club behind the ball and tell me how far away the hole is. Then I swing.

12 Trying something you've never done before definitely can be scary. But that's true whether you're blind or sighted. My thinking is, you can't say no until you try. There's always a way to do whatever it is that you want to do.

> **adapt**   If you adapt to something, you figure out how to deal with it.

The red binders are printed in braille. It takes all those to equal one math book.

If you see someone with a guide dog…

🐾 If the dog has on a harness, like the one Twyla is wearing, that means the dog is working. So treat it like anyone who has a job to do: with respect.

✋ Don't pet the dog unless the owner says it's OK.

🎾 Be cool: Don't bark at or tease the dog, or try to distract it.

🚶 It's OK to ask a person with a dog if he needs help crossing the street. Just don't grab his arm and drag him across!

🦴 Never feed the dog.

Twyla came to me through Guide Dogs for the Blind, which trains dogs to help people like me. Unfortunately, the dogs aren't trained to play golf!

MY BEST FRIEND

13   Now, I accept that I can't do everything on my own, even with Twyla's help. I have to be OK with asking people to help me cross busy streets. Other times I need someone to read me something because it's not in Braille. It can be hard to ask for help, but if I don't, I can't live my life.

14   When things do get too hard—like when I want to go to the golf course but there's no one to drive me, or when some kid says, "Catch," then throws something at my head—that's when Twyla steps in to comfort me. I just pet her and talk to her. She's that friend that's always there, and she reminds me that, yeah, things are hard sometimes . . . but they'll get better.

15   I just look at it this way: There's always something life takes from you, and something life gives back. Like, I think being blind makes me a better golfer. Sighted golfers will lift their heads to watch their shot, and that messes with their swing. But I can't see the ball, so I don't do that.

16   I may never compete against a pro golfer. Then again, it could happen.

17   I'd just make him wear a blindfold.

> **comfort**   If you comfort someone, you say or do things to make the person feel better.

To help me play golf, my dad or coach places the club behind the ball. Then they tell me which way to swing.

Collaborative Discussion

Look back at what you wrote on page 132. Tell a partner two things you learned about Matthew. Then work with a group to discuss the questions below. Look for details in *Blind Ambition* to support your ideas. Take notes for your responses. When you speak, use your notes. Be sure to follow your class rules for having a good discussion.

1. Reread pages 134–135. What words and actions in the text show Matthew's relationship with Twyla?

> There a team

2. Review pages 136–138. What details in the text and photos show ways in which Matthew has adapted to his blindness?

> He knows what to do in asitiation

3. What details in the text show what Matthew is like?

> nice and try to do everything kid

Listening Tip

Listen attentively to each speaker. Wait until the speaker has finished before adding your own ideas.

Speaking Tip

If you disagree with another speaker, do so politely. Explain how evidence from the text supports your own point of view or opinion.

Write a Journal Entry

In *Blind Ambition,* you read about how Matthew has adapted so he can live and enjoy life. Much of the text is organized by stating a central idea followed by supporting details.

Imagine that you are Matthew. Write a journal entry about your day. Use details from the text to tell about how being blind affected your activities and the role that Twyla played in your day. Don't forget to use some of the Critical Vocabulary words in your writing.

PLAN

Make notes of words and phrases that show things Matthew likes to do. Then, choose one activity and write details from the text that tell how Matthew adapts that activity.

WRITE

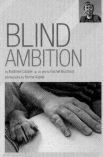

Now write your journal entry about Matthew's day.

✓ | **Make sure your journal entry**

☐ uses first-person pronouns, such as *I*, *me*, *my*, and *myself*.

☐ includes details from the text to describe Matthew's day.

☐ has a structure that clearly explains Matthew's day.

☐ uses verbs correctly.

☐ ends with a concluding statement.

Prepare to Read

GENRE STUDY **Historical fiction** is a story that is set in a real time and place in the past.

- Historical fiction includes characters who act, think, and speak like real people from the past would.
- Authors of historical fiction tell the story through the plot—the main events of the story.
- Authors of historical fiction may use figurative language to develop the setting and the characters.

SET A PURPOSE **Look at** the picture on the next page. Think about what it reveals about the characters. What do you want to learn about these characters? Write your ideas below.

**Meet the Author:
Louise Erdrich**

CRITICAL VOCABULARY

absurd

taunt

forfeit

despised

ferocious

elaborately

coveted

THE GAME OF SILENCE

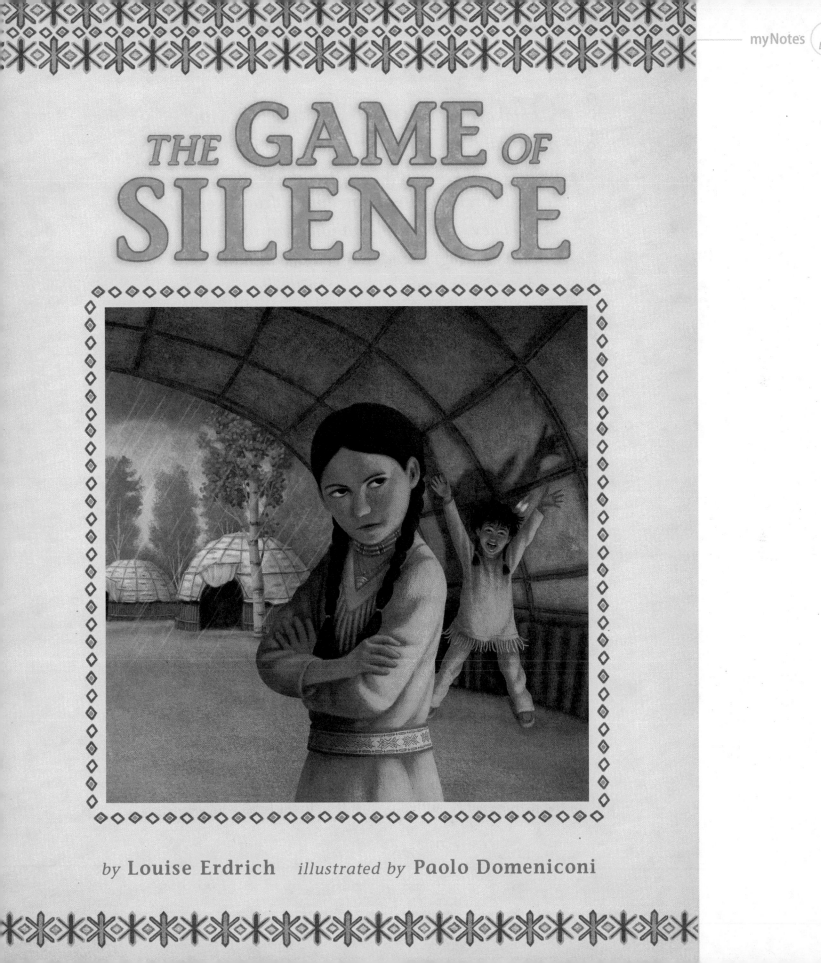

by **Louise Erdrich**   illustrated by **Paolo Domeniconi**

1 *Omakayas is an Ojibwe girl who lives with her family on Lake Superior. It is 1850, and members of a neighboring tribe have just recently arrived after being forced from their land. They have traveled a long way and they are tired, hungry, and "raggedy." Omakayas and her brother are at home with their grandmother, Nokomis. They begin to play a silent game while they wait for others to arrive so the adults can discuss what is happening to their people.*

2 Words. Words. Words. Pressing up from her stomach, trembling on her lips. Words buzzing in her throat like caught bees. Banging in her head. Harsh words. Angry words. Sounds boiling up in her like sap. Wild things she couldn't let out.

3 Yow! A kick from her brother almost caused Omakayas to blurt an exclamation.

4 No! Omakayas sealed her lips together in a firm line and glared at her brother with all of the force pent up inside. If the fire from her eyes could scorch him, Pinch would be the first to yell out. Then he would lose the game of silence. But Pinch was used to receiving furious looks from his family. He knew just how to respond. First he looked innocently at Omakayas (as though he was *ever* innocent!). He pretended he was unaware of the raging energy stuffed up inside of his sister. Then, as

◇◇◇◇◇◇◇◇◇◇◇◇◇◇◇◇◇◇◇◇◇◇◇◇◇◇◇◇◇◇◇◇◇

Omakayas bored her eyes at him with increasing intensity, he lolled out his tongue and twisted his face into a deranged and awful mask. His features shifted into one ugly and absurd face after the next until suddenly Omakayas just about . . . almost . . . laughed. Just in time, she clapped her hand to her mouth. Closed her eyes. Concentrated. Yes. Eya'[1]. She would be a stone. Asineeg[2]. A pile of stones. Each one harder and quieter than the next. She would be silent and more silent yet. And in spite of her annoying brother, she would win. She kept her eyes closed, put her forehead on her knees. Thought stone, stone, stone. Asin[3]. Asin. Filled her mind with the sound of falling rain, which was easy. Outside, it was not just raining but *pouring* down a drenching, cold, miserable, early summer shower.

1 **eya' (ey-ah):** yes
2 **asineeg (ah-sin-ig):** a pile of stones
3 **asin (ah-sin):** stone

absurd   If something is absurd, you think it is silly or ridiculous.

✳

5   The rain had lasted for days, since the raggedy ones arrived.
That was another thing. Besides Pinch, Omakayas couldn't stand
rain anymore. The water made mush of tender new ground
around her family's birchbark house. Droplets hissed through
the roof vent into the fire, driving stinging smoke into her eyes.
Everyone around her was affected. Nokomis's old bones ached,
and she creaked like a tree every time she moved. The watery
wind sent coughs racking through her mother's chest. It was too
wet to play outside, and cold when it should have been warm.
Worst of all, Omakayas was stuck with Pinch.

6   He nudged her. Omakayas almost slugged him in return, but
controlled herself. She'd had enough of him to last her whole
life! She opened her eyes a fraction, then her eyes went wide in
shock. Somehow, Pinch had got hold of her beloved doll, and he
was making it teeter on the cliff of his knees. Omakayas bit her
lip so hard it hurt. Pinch walked her doll to the edge of his
knees, then teasingly back. If only Mama was here! If only she
would return! Nokomis concentrated on her work so hard it
was impossible to distract her.

7   Omakayas pretended to shut her eyes again, but cleverly
watched until just the right moment to snatch back her doll. She
sighed as though she was falling asleep and then, with a flash,
she grabbed. Taken by surprise, Pinch couldn't react quickly
enough to hold on, and Omakayas triumphantly clutched her
doll. She stuck it down the neck of her dress. There! Safe! Inside,
she laughed, but she didn't make a single sound, not a chirp, not
so much as a mouse's squeak.

✳

8   She was going to win the game of silence, she just knew it. Pinch was now poking little twigs into the fire in the center fire pit, watching them burn. Omakayas tried not to notice him, but his head was so big and fuzzy. Pinch's hair sprang out with its own energy. Crafty eyes in his rough, round face calculated his sister's endurance. He was surely cooking up some mischief. Sure enough, Pinch drew the burning wand from the fire and laid it innocently next to her ankle—as though she didn't know that it would scorch her if she moved the slightest inch! And make her cry out, first, and instantly lose the game! She kicked it back at him.

9   "Gego[4], Pinch," she nearly warned, but bit her lip.

10   "Eah, eah, eah," he mouthed the taunt, making an impossibly irritating face that almost broke Omakayas's discipline.

4 **gego (GAY-go):** exclamation meaning "stop that"

taunt   A taunt is something someone says to anger or upset someone else.

◈■◆│◈■◆│◈■◆│◈■◆│◈■◆│◈■◆│◈■◆│◈■◆│◈■◆

11   Luckily, just at the second that Omakayas decided to forfeit the game and to smash her little brother over the head with the big tin soup ladle, the visitors arrived.

12   "They are here," said their grandmother. "You can quit the game until after we eat."

forfeit If you forfeit something, you lose it because you have broken a rule.

13   "Aaaagh!" Omakayas exploded with such a wild sound of rage that Nokomis jumped. Pinch retreated, unnerved by how sorely he'd tested his sister. Omakayas breathed out in relief. These visitors were her friends and cousins—Twilight, Little Bee, and Two Strike Girl. They had brought the boy she called, in her mind, the Angry One. Her cousins were her favorite friends, the ones she counted on. Twilight was much like her name, quiet and thoughtful. Little Bee was funny and bold. Two Strike was tough and she could do anything a boy could do, usually better. Since her mother had died, she was wilder than ever. Even her father had not been able to handle Two Strike, and had left her with Auntie Muskrat. But Auntie Muskrat had had no success in taming Two Strike. Sometimes she was so fierce that she outdid everyone—it was a challenge to play with her. The girls had learned to sew and bead together, gathered berries, and helped their mothers clean fish. They also learned early on how to tan hides, a task that Omakayas despised. And now too, her sister, Angeline, was home. Omakayas grinned with satisfaction. Pinch was delightfully outnumbered by girls and would pout, creeping to Mama's side when she arrived, and turning into a baby, hoping to be pampered with tidbits of meat and maple sugar.

> **despised**   If you despised something, you felt a strong dislike for it.

151

14   Now everyone—the children and their parents—squeezed into the lodge. They had made the lodge extra big that summer, for visitors. For the first time, it was packed entirely full, but there was enough room for everyone. Even the Angry One found a space to sit. He glared from a little spot against the wall. Together, they ate rich venison soup from the shallow birchbark makakoon[5] they'd brought along with them. Two other men squeezed in, important men. Old Tallow entered, huge and rangy and smelling of wolf. She settled herself while outside her ferocious dogs stood guard, unmoving and alert even in the pelting rain. Each of Old Tallow's feet seemed to take up as much space as a small child, but Omakayas didn't mind. Warily, but completely, she loved the fierce old woman.

5 makakoon (mah-kah-koon): containers of birchbark folded and often stitched together with basswood fiber

ferocious Something that is ferocious is very fierce, mean, and violent.

15   Each visitor brought a gift for the pile that the children who won the game of silence would choose from that night. For it was an important night. With the raggedy ones came serious doings. Difficult questions and impossible news. Great attention was needed. The grown-ups needed to council, think, absorb the facts, without having to shush small children. The children could tell how important the meeting was from the degree to which their silence was required. The pile of treats was the best ever.

16   There was a bag of marbles, some of actual glass, not just clay. A pair of narrow makazinan that Omakayas thought just might fit her. One doll, elaborately dressed in a tiny set of britches and a leather coat. A sharp knife. A deer knuckle game. Two duck's bills of maple sugar tied together with split jack-pine root. Six red ribbons. A little roll of flowered cloth. Eight tiny bells. One small bow, and six arrows tipped with real brass points cut from a trade kettle. The arrows were fletched with the sharp black and yellow feathers of a bird that the island where they lived was named for—the golden-breasted woodpecker. Old Tallow must have brought them. What treasures! The children examined them breathlessly, each picking out one particular prize they meant to win.

> **elaborately**   If something is elaborately dressed or decorated, it has many complex artistic details.

17   Little Bee, of course, wanted the doll. Two Strike Girl, the bow and arrows. Pinch coveted the knife, but he was torn by greed for the maple sugar and the need for marbles to replace those he'd lost. The Angry One did not deign to move from his spot or look at the gifts. No doubt he'd have no problem winning the game! As for Twilight, quiet and serene, she had no trouble playing the game and she would be content with anything. Omakayas wanted the ribbons, the bells, and the marbles, too, but she settled on the makazinan because she had watched her grandmother make them so carefully. They were fancy, with velvet ankle cuffs, the tops beaded with flowers and little white sparkling vines. Worth her silence!

18   Now the grown-ups were ready to start talking. Nokomis sang the song of the game of silence four times, nearly catching Pinch at the end. Then she turned away from them too, absorbed in the talk.

coveted   If you coveted something, you wanted it very much.

19   Omakayas looked longingly at Twilight, and her cousin made a sad and frustrated face. With her favorite cousin so close and her annoying brother so near, it was difficult to play. If only they could talk! At first, the girls communicated by mouthing words and moving their eyes, but the temptation to laugh was too great. They turned away from each other unwillingly. Omakayas listened to the rain, a solid drumming and hissing. Then she listened to the fire crackling and sighing. She watched the beautiful and changing glow of the coals. At some point, Omakayas couldn't tell exactly when, her attention was caught by something her father said. And then she noticed that her cousin Twilight was also listening to the grown-ups' conversation. Soon, they all couldn't help but listen. They leaned forward, straining to hear every sound, almost forgetting to breathe.

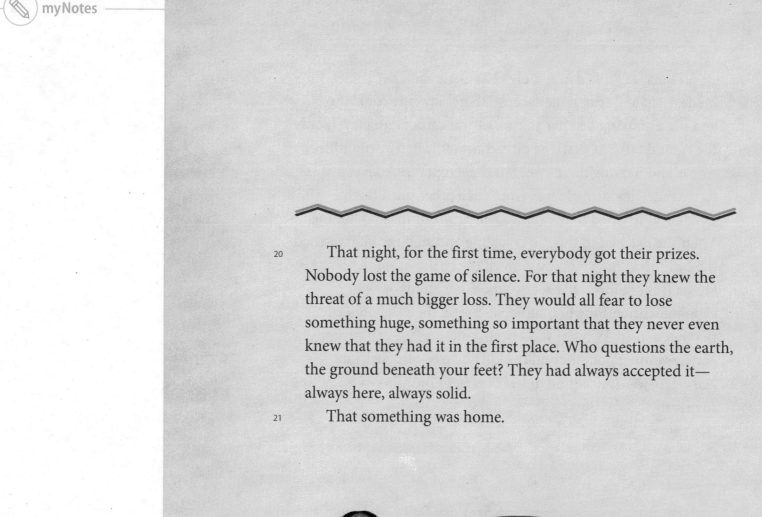

20   That night, for the first time, everybody got their prizes. Nobody lost the game of silence. For that night they knew the threat of a much bigger loss. They would all fear to lose something huge, something so important that they never even knew that they had it in the first place. Who questions the earth, the ground beneath your feet? They had always accepted it— always here, always solid.

21   That something was home.

Collaborative Discussion

Look back at what you wrote on page 142. Tell a partner two things you learned about the characters in the story. Then work with a group to discuss the questions below. Refer to details and examples in *The Game of Silence* to explain your answers. Be an active listener and ask questions that help your group stay on topic.

1 Reread pages 144–145. What does Omakayas do to help her stay silent?

2 Review pages 153–154. Who plays the game of silence? Why is the game being played?

3 What details show that the night is important to Omakayas and her family?

Listening Tip

Listen closely and focus on what each speaker says. What is his or her main idea?

Speaking Tip

Remind others of the topic by restating the idea the group is discussing. Then ask the group a question about that topic.

Write an Informative Paragraph

In *The Game of Silence,* you read about a group of children in an Ojibwe tribe who played a silent game while their families had a meeting. The story events were told in sequential order.

Imagine that you are writing part of a report on Ojibwe culture. Use details from the story to write an informative paragraph that explains how to play the game played by the children in *The Game of Silence.* Don't forget to use some of the Critical Vocabulary words in your writing.

PLAN

Make notes about the rules of the game of silence. Then underline the important events in the story.

WRITE

Now write your informative paragraph explaining how to play the game of silence.

✓	Make sure your informative paragraph
☐	has a clear topic sentence.
☐	uses facts and other information from the text.
☐	uses precise language and vocabulary to explain the rules of the game.
☐	uses complete sentences.
☐	ends with a concluding sentence.

(?) **Essential Question**

How do people and animals use their senses to navigate the world?

Write an Informative Article

PROMPT Think about what you learned about the five senses in this module.

Imagine you are in the Science Club at school and have volunteered to write an article for the club's newsletter. Use evidence from the texts and video to explain how one sense helps people and animals to survive and navigate the world.

I will write about the sense of _____.

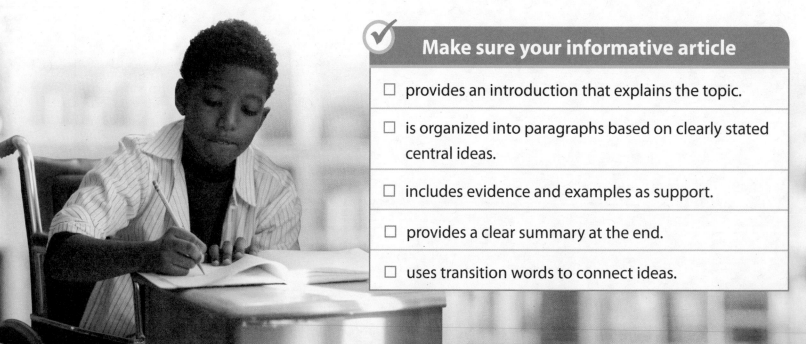

✓ **Make sure your informative article**

- ☐ provides an introduction that explains the topic.
- ☐ is organized into paragraphs based on clearly stated central ideas.
- ☐ includes evidence and examples as support.
- ☐ provides a clear summary at the end.
- ☐ uses transition words to connect ideas.

What ideas about your choice of sense will you write about? Look back at your notes, and revisit the texts and video as necessary.

In the chart below, write a central, or main, idea. Then use evidence from the texts and video to write supporting details. Use Critical Vocabulary words where appropriate.

My Topic: _____

Central Idea

Detail

Detail

Detail

DRAFT ·· Write your article.

Write an **introduction** that will grab readers' attention and clearly state your overall central idea.

For the **body paragraph**, refer to your chart to help you write a central idea sentence and supporting sentences.

In your **conclusion**, restate your overall central idea.

REVISE AND EDIT ··· Review your draft.

The revision and editing steps give you a chance to look carefully at your writing and make changes. Work with a partner to determine whether you have explained your ideas clearly to readers. Use these questions to help you evaluate and improve your article.

PURPOSE/ FOCUS	ORGANIZATION	EVIDENCE	LANGUAGE/ VOCABULARY	CONVENTIONS
☐ Does my article state a clear central idea? ☐ Have I stayed on topic?	☐ Will my introduction grab readers' attention? ☐ Have I provided a strong conclusion?	☐ Does the evidence I chose support my central idea?	☐ Did I use signal words and linking words to create a smooth flow of ideas?	☐ Have I used proper spelling? ☐ Have I used verbs correctly? ☐ Did I indent each new paragraph?

PUBLISH ·································· Share your work.

Create a Finished Copy Make a final copy of your informative article. You may wish to include a photo or illustration. Consider these options to share your article:

1. Collect your classmates' articles and bind them in a science newsletter.

2. Publish your article on a school website or social networking page, and ask for feedback from readers.

3. Share your article in a classroom panel discussion about the senses.

Rise to the Occasion

"When we least expect it, life sets us a challenge to test our courage and willingness to change."

—Paulo Coelho

? Essential Question

What does it take to meet a challenge?

Get Curious

Video

Words About Rising to the Occasion

The words in the chart will help you talk and write about the selections in this module. Which words about rising to the occasion or meeting challenges have you seen before? Which words are new to you?

Add to the Vocabulary Network on page 167 by writing synonyms, antonyms, and related words and phrases for each word about rising to the occasion.

After you read each selection in this module, come back to the Vocabulary Network and keep building it. Add more ovals if you need to.

WORD	MEANING	CONTEXT SENTENCE
confront (verb)	When you confront a problem, you deal with that problem.	It takes courage to confront a difficult situation.
dauntless (adjective)	Someone who is dauntless has no fears.	The dauntless firefighter ran into the burning house to save the family.
endurance (noun)	If you have endurance, you can do something for a long time.	Running marathons requires endurance and strength.
dedication (noun)	If someone has dedication for something, that person has shown a commitment to it.	Maria spends every weekend cleaning up the park, showing her dedication to her community.

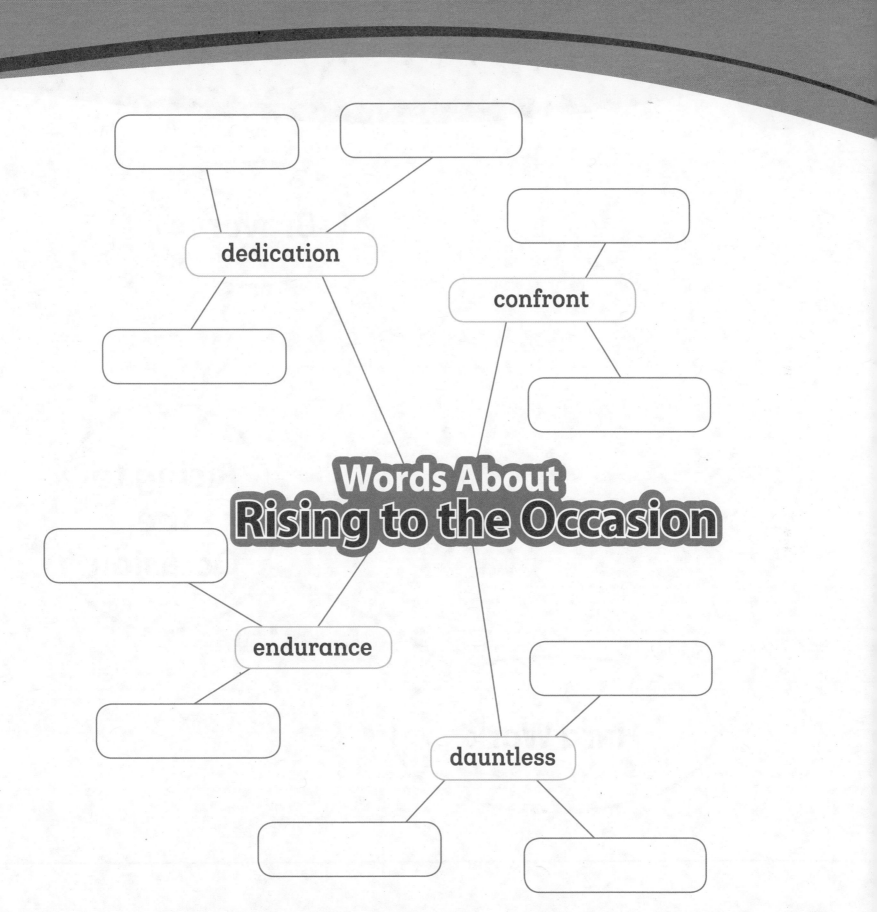

dedication

confront

Words About
Rising to the Occasion

endurance

dauntless

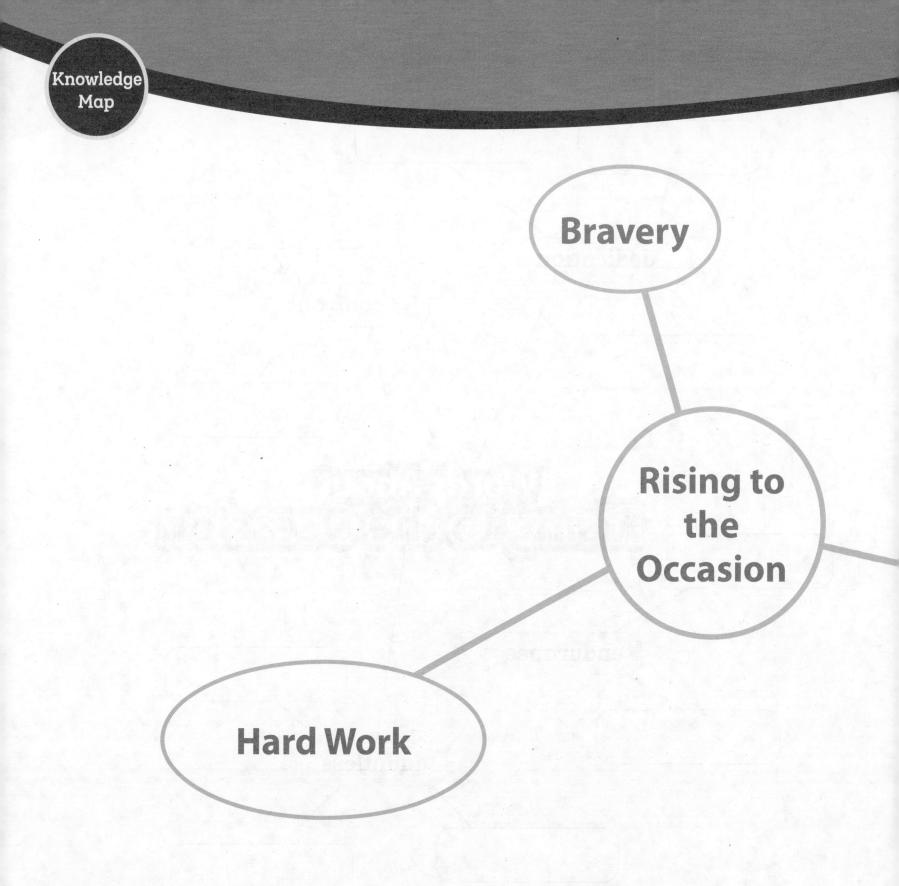

Bravery

Rising to
the
Occasion

Hard Work

Persistence

NEVER GIVE UP!

1 From taking a test to climbing a mountain, life is all about facing challenges. At times these challenges can seem overwhelming. You may want to back down or run as fast as you can in the other direction. Here's why you shouldn't.

Persistence Pays Off

2 When you work to meet a challenge, you get stronger, smarter, and braver. You have to, because challenges require hard work and endurance. They make you push yourself beyond what comes easily to you. You learn, practice, and build the skills you need to get the job done. Doing all this doesn't just help you meet a particular challenge. It makes you more prepared for the next one, and it builds the kind of confidence that lets you say, "I've got this!"

3 Speaking of being prepared for a challenge, be sure to do your research. Get tips from others who have succeeded at the same task. Find out what they did to get ready, and learn what obstacles they faced on the way to success. This knowledge will give you a head start and increase your odds of succeeding.

Giving Up Is a Bad Habit

4 There's another important reason to confront challenges. Backing down can become a habit—not the good kind, like flossing or making your bed, but the bad kind, like biting your nails. It's tempting to think giving up "just this once" is no big deal, but when you do, it's easier to give up the next time.

5 Instead of giving up, be dauntless. Tell yourself you won't quit no matter what. Tell yourself the task is worth doing. Tell yourself you can do it with focus and dedication. Think about how good you'll feel if you achieve your goal, and picture that success in your mind.

Challenge Yourself to Grow

6 It's important to keep something else in mind, too. Success won't always be the outcome. Sometimes we try our best and still fail to achieve a goal. Believe it or not, that's another reason to persist when you face challenges. Failure helps you learn and grow and get stronger, maybe even more than success does! When you fail at a challenge, what matters is trying again. Keep in mind that others value your efforts, no matter what the outcome—and you should, too.

7 Working hard and not giving up teaches you courage. The more courage you have, the more you believe in yourself, and that leads to success! So whatever you do, keep on going. Rise to the next challenge. There's no stopping you!

Prepare to Read

GENRE STUDY ▸ **Historical fiction** is a story that is set in a real time and place in the past.

- Characters in historical fiction stories act, think, and speak like real people from the past would.
- Characters may use slang that was common during the time period.
- Authors of historical fiction might tell the story through third-person point of view. In third-person point of view, the story is told through an outside observer.

SET A PURPOSE ▸ **Look through** the text and the illustrations. What do you notice about the people and places shown? What would you like to know about them? Write your ideas below.

CRITICAL VOCABULARY

auction

drifting

damp

spare

verses

chorus

brimming

Written by:
William Miller
Illustrated by:
Charlotte Riley-Webb

RENT PARTY JAZZ

by **William Miller**

illustrated by **Charlotte Riley-Webb**

1   **E**very morning, as the sun was coming up, Sonny went to work for the coal man. "I sells mah coal two bits a sack," the coal man cried out as they drove slowly down the streets of the French Quarter.

2   Sonny wished he were back in his warm bed, but he knew how badly he and Mama needed the extra money. Even though he would spend the rest of the day in school, Sonny started the day like a working man.

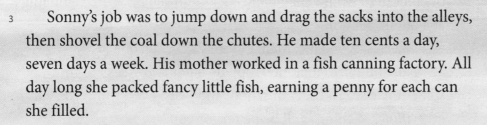

3   Sonny's job was to jump down and drag the sacks into the alleys, then shovel the coal down the chutes. He made ten cents a day, seven days a week. His mother worked in a fish canning factory. All day long she packed fancy little fish, earning a penny for each can she filled.

4   When Sonny and the coal man drove through Jackson Square, they would hear trumpet players blowing their horns. The musicians played any tune people wanted to hear, hoping listeners would drop a few coins into their hats.

5 One morning Sonny came home to find Mama sitting at the kitchen table. She looked like she had been crying.

6 "What's the matter, Mama?" Sonny asked. "Are you sick?"

7 "Worse than sick, Sonny. I've been let go from my job. These are some hard times, and folks aren't buyin' much fancy fish. Might be three, four months 'fore they need these hands again."

8 Sonny's heart sank. Rent day would be coming soon, and the rent man didn't care whether you had a job or not. All he wanted was his money. If they missed paying the rent by just one day, the rent man would change the locks and sell off their belongings at a public auction.

9 "I'll get a second job, Mama," Sonny said. "I'll quit . . ."

10 "No, Sonny," Mama interrupted. "I got two weeks to find somethin' else. You stay in school and learn everything you can— *everything*, so things will be better for you."

11 After school that day, Sonny wandered through the streets of the Quarter, tired and sad. There had to be something he could do to help raise the rent money.

auction An auction is an event where items are sold to the person who offers the most money.

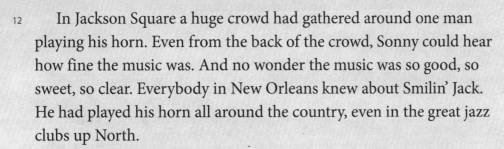

12   In Jackson Square a huge crowd had gathered around one man
playing his horn. Even from the back of the crowd, Sonny could hear
how fine the music was. And no wonder the music was so good, so
sweet, so clear. Everybody in New Orleans knew about Smilin' Jack.
He had played his horn all around the country, even in the great jazz
clubs up North.

13   Smilin' Jack looked like the happiest man in the world, blowing
his magic horn, collecting bucketfuls of coins. He seemed so happy,
Sonny felt even worse about Mama and the rent money.

14   The next day and the next, Sonny found himself back in Jackson Square after school. Smilin' Jack's music was too good to ignore. Sonny always stood toward the front of the crowd, though he still felt too sad and worried to clap or sing along. On the third day Sonny stayed until the music was over and people began drifting from the Square.

15   "Hey, young man, what's your name?" Smilin' Jack asked as he stepped down from the platform.

16   "Sonny Comeaux, sir."

17   "You need a special tune, Sonny? You're looking mighty down. Sure wish I could get those hands clapping."

18   "I love your music, Smilin' Jack," Sonny said. "But a tune won't solve my problems."

19   "Problems? What kind of problems does a boy like you have?"

20   Sonny explained about his mother losing her job, about the rent man who'd put them out on the street if they missed paying the rent.

21   Smilin' Jack suddenly looked serious. "Back in Mississippi, where I come from, they did the same thing to colored folks all the time.

---

drifting   If you are drifting, you are moving slowly without much direction.

But then we found a new way to fight back, pay the rent man, and have the world's best party at the same time."

22   "How'd you do that?" Sonny asked.

23   "All the neighbors got together and threw themselves a rent party," Smilin' Jack said. "They baked sweet potato pies, fixed up some catfish and greens, then brought the food to the house where help was needed. They put out a big empty bucket, too, and soon someone who knew how to pluck a fine banjo or blow a jazz horn would start playing—make people sing and dance and forget their worries for a while. By the end of the night, people had dropped enough money in that bucket to put the old rent man back in his place."

24   "That sounds like a mighty fine idea," Sonny said. "But where am I going to find somebody who'll play for Mama and me, play for poor people he doesn't even know?"

25   Smilin' Jack faked a frown and tapped his foot. "Some people say I play a pretty mean trumpet myself."

26   For the first time in days, Sonny smiled.

27   When Sonny got home, he found Mama sitting near the stove.

28   "No luck again today, Sonny," she said. "But I'll keep lookin'. I'll find me that job to keep us goin'."

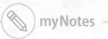

29   Sonny stirred the coals with a poker, trying to warm the damp room.

30   "Maybe you won't need that job right away, Mama," Sonny said. "We're going to have a party tonight and raise all the money we need for the rent, every last nickel and dime. Smilin' Jack told me how to do it."

31   "Don't be talking such foolishness, Sonny, even if you're just tryin' to cheer me up," Mama said, pulling her shawl tighter around her shoulders.

32   "It's not foolishness, Mama," Sonny insisted. "I'm going to prove it to you."

33   Sonny knocked on all the neighbors' doors, told them about the party and asked them to bring whatever food they could spare. He told them to get ready for the best music in the world. They were all going to meet the great Smilin' Jack!

34   On his way home, Sonny found an empty bucket in an alley. He put it on the floor just inside the doorway and sat down beside Mama to wait. Mama shook her head, thinking her poor son had just plain lost his mind.

damp   If something is damp, it feels a little wet.

spare   Something you can spare is something extra that you have and that you don't really need.

35   A little while later Sonny and Mama heard cheering and clapping in the street. Then someone knocked loudly on the door.

36   "Mrs. Comeaux, I sure am pleased to meet you." Smilin' Jack, trumpet in hand, bowed to Mama.

37   "Well, I'll be! I thought my boy had gone full-moon crazy," Mama said, hardly believing her eyes. "I sure love your music, Smilin' Jack. I surely do."

38   Before Mama could say another word, Smilin' Jack pulled the bucket toward him, raised his trumpet, and started blowing one of Sonny's favorite songs, "Bourbon Street Rag."

39   The house and the street were soon filled with people. There was more food than Sonny had ever seen at one time, enough for everyone who was busy clapping and singing and dancing.

40   All the neighbors had come to the party! Sonny saw the LeBlanc twins running through the crowd. And he saw the oldest woman in the neighborhood, Mrs. Clairveaux, sitting in a chair, tapping along to the music with her cane.

41   Just one thing bothered Sonny at first. He heard only a few coins drop into the bucket. But as the night went on and the party heated up, he heard more and more and more.

42   At last Smilin' Jack stopped playing. Then, without any music, he started singing "When the Saints Go Marching In." The whole crowd joined in, singing the verses, then the beautiful chorus.

43   Sonny felt like he was in another world, a place where the music and the singing he loved would never stop.

44   When everyone had left, the bucket was brimming with coins. Mama counted out the money they needed for the rent and handed the rest to Smilin' Jack.

45   "I thank you much, Smilin' Jack," she said. "I took what I need to see us through. This belongs to you."

46   Smilin' Jack shook his head. "No ma'am. That money belongs to anybody who needs it for rent or food. I've already been paid. This was the most fun I've had in a long time. Wherever I go from now on, I'm going to play at least one rent party like this. We'll show those rent men how good folks help each other."

47   Sonny walked Smilin' Jack back to Jackson Square.

48   "Thank you, Sonny Comeaux, for one of the happiest nights of my life," Smilin' Jack said. "I sure hope to see you the next time I come to town. I know just where to find you now." They shook hands and hugged like old friends.

---

verses The verses of a song are the different sections that usually change throughout the song.

chorus The chorus of a song is the part that is repeated after each verse.

brimming If something is brimming, it is full and about to overflow.

49   Sonny walked home slowly, wishing the night would never end. He was glad he had listened to Mama. If he had quit school and taken a second job, he would never have met Smilin' Jack, never have learned about bringing the neighbors together for a rent party. It made him think about how much people could do for one another if they put their minds and hearts to it.

50   Sonny figured he would stay in school and learn everything in his books and lessons. And maybe, just maybe, he'd learn to play the trumpet, too.

51   Beneath the bright glow of the street lamps, Sonny swayed back and forth, pretending he could blow a mean horn.

Collaborative Discussion

Look back at what you wrote on page 172. Tell a partner two things you learned about the characters and setting. Then work with a group to discuss the questions below. Support your answers with details and examples from *Rent Party Jazz*. Take notes for your responses. Use your notes when you speak.

1 Reread page 176. What problem do Sonny and Mama have? How do they think they might solve it?

2 Review pages 178–179. How does Smilin' Jack help solve Sonny and Mama's problem?

3 How are Sonny and Smilin' Jack alike? How are they different?

Listening Tip

Listen carefully to each person. Wait until a speaker has finished talking before adding your own thoughts.

Speaking Tip

You might notice that someone in your group hasn't said anything yet. After explaining your ideas, you can ask that person what he or she thinks about what you said.

Write a Thank-You Note

PROMPT ....

In *Rent Party Jazz,* you read about how Smilin' Jack and members of the community come together to help Sonny and his family. The story's setting and characters show how it takes place in the past.

Imagine that you are Sonny. Write Smilin' Jack a thank-you note for his help. Use descriptive language to tell about your feelings and how he helped solve your problem. Don't forget to use some of the Critical Vocabulary in your writing.

PLAN ....

Write down the problem that Smilin' Jack helped solve. Then take notes about how the the historical setting affects the events in the plot.

WRITE

Now write your thank-you note from Sonny to Smilin' Jack.

Make sure your thank-you note

- ☐ begins with a greeting.
- ☐ explains why you are thanking Smilin' Jack.
- ☐ uses events from the text.
- ☐ ends with a concluding statement.
- ☐ uses verb tenses correctly.

Notice & Note
Quoted Words

Prepare to Read

GENRE STUDY ▶ **Narrative nonfiction** gives factual information by telling a true story about people, places, or events. **Personal narratives** tell about an important event in a real person's life.

- Authors of narrative nonfiction and personal narratives present events in sequential, or chronological, order.
- Narrative nonfiction tells about events from the past. Events are told from a secondhand point of view.
- Personal narratives give a firsthand account about an experience.

SET A PURPOSE ▶ **Look at** the photograph on the next page. This text describes events that happened in 1900. What do you want to learn about this event? Write your ideas below.

▶ Build Background: Hurricanes

CRITICAL VOCABULARY

surge

perished

debris

THE GALVESTON HURRICANE
★ of 1900 ★

Galveston, Texas before the storm hit

1 In 1900, Galveston, Texas, was a busy commercial port. It was also a popular place to vacation. The city sat just along the Gulf of Mexico. Warm waters lapped along its beaches. It would have been an ideal place to visit at the time. But Galveston was on a barrier island. Barrier islands can slow down storms approaching the mainland. They take the impact of the damaging winds and storm surge that accompany a hurricane. This was Galveston's fate.

2 A few days before the "Great Storm," scientists predicted the storm's path would go along the East Coast of the United States. Unfortunately for the 38,000 residents of Texas, the storm changed direction. On September 8, 1900, the hurricane struck.

★ THE STORM'S ARRIVAL ★

3 The ocean swelled. Waves rose twenty feet within hours. The storm surge easily flooded the island that Galveston called home. Wind speeds grew to 135 miles per hour. It was a Category 4 hurricane, the worst natural disaster in U.S. history.

4 Buildings were shattered from the storm's force. They washed up near other collapsed buildings. People who hid in these structures were crushed. Other people drowned. The storm wiped out entire blocks and destroyed about 3,600 homes. About 8,000 people perished in the storm.

surge   If there is a surge of water, there is a sudden large increase in its depth.
perished   When people or animals perished, they died.

5   *Milton Elford was a young man living in Galveston with his mother, father, and a young nephew, Dwight. Milton was the only member of his family to survive the storm. He described his experience in a letter to his brothers in North Dakota. This portion of his letter begins as the rising water and intensity of the storm persuade the family to leave their home for a sturdier brick house across the street.*

6   "We left our house about 4 o'clock thinking we would be safer in a larger house, not dreaming that even that house would be washed away. We went across the street to a fine large house, built on a brick foundation high off the ground. About 5 it grew worse and began to break up the fence, and the wreckage of other houses was coming against us.

Galveston was a busy commercial port before the storm.

Galveston after the storm. Approximately 3,600 homes were destroyed.

7   We had arranged that if the house showed signs of breaking up, I would take the lead and Pa would come next, with Dwight and Ma next. In this way I could make a safe place to walk, as we would have to depend on floating debris for rafts.

8   There were about fifteen or sixteen in the house besides ourselves. They were confident the house would stand anything; if not for that we would probably have left on rafts before the house went down. We all gathered in one room; all at once the house went from its foundation and the water came in waist-deep, and we all made a break for the door, but could not get it open. We then smashed out the window and I led the way.

9   I had only got part way out when the house fell on us. I was hit on the head with something and it knocked me out and into the water head first. I do not know how long I was down, as I must have been stunned. I came up and got hold of some wreckage on the other side of the house. I could see one man on some wreckage to my left and another on my right. I went back to the door that we could not open. It was broke in, and I could go part way in, as one side of the ceiling was not within four or five feet, I think, of water. There was not a thing in sight.

debris   Debris is the pieces of something that was broken or destroyed.

10   . . . I went back and got on the other side but no one ever came up that I could see. We must all have gone down the same time, but I cannot tell [why] they did not come up.

11   I then started to leave by partly running and swimming from one lot of debris to another. The street was full of tops and sides of houses and the air was full of flying boards. I think I gained about a block on the debris in this way, and got in the shelter of some buildings, but they were fast going down, and I was afraid of getting buried.

12   Just then, the part I was on started down the street, and I stuck my head and shoulders in an old tool chest that was lying in the debris that I was on. I could hardly hold this down on its side from being blown away, but that is what saved my life again.

13   When the water went down about 3 a.m., I was about five blocks from where I started. My head was bruised and legs and hands cut a little, which I did not find until Monday and then I could hardly get my hat on.

14   . . . As soon as it was light enough, I went back to the location of the house, and not a sign of it could be found and not a sign [of] any house within two blocks, where before there was scarcely a vacant lot."

The storm shattered buildings and destroyed entire blocks of homes.

★ AFTER THE STORM ★

15 **The storm passed** in the early morning hours of the next day. The residents of Galveston began the task of cleaning up the wreckage and rebuilding the city. These efforts included raising the buildings up to 17 feet by pumping sand beneath the foundations. A sturdy seawall was built along the ocean front. But what was once the busiest seaport in Texas was forever changed. The devastating storm convinced shippers to move north to Houston. It took over a decade for Galveston to fully rebuild and become the thriving city it once was.

The city of Galveston today

Collaborative Discussion

Look back at what you wrote on page 190. Tell a partner two things you learned from the text. Then work with a group to discuss the questions below. Provide support for your answers using details from *The Galveston Hurricane of 1900*.

1 Reread page 192. Why weren't the people of Galveston prepared for the hurricane?

2 Review page 193. What details show that the Elford family's plan to go to the house across the street made sense?

3 How is the information in each account of the hurricane similar? How is it different?

Listening Tip

Notice the reasons and evidence that each speaker provides. Decide if you agree with those reasons.

Speaking Tip

Tell which ideas you agree with and which you disagree with. Be sure to explain why!

Write a News Story

PROMPT ....

In *The Galveston Hurricane of 1900,* you read what happened when a powerful storm struck the city of Galveston, Texas. The text presented the events from both first-person and third-person points of view.

Imagine that you are a newspaper reporter in 1900. Write a front-page story for your newspaper telling about the Galveston hurricane. Don't forget to use some of the Critical Vocabulary words in your writing.

PLAN ....

Write the following: *Who? When? Where? What? Why?* and *How?* Then use the question words to make notes about the hurricane. Remember that you will be telling the story from a third-person point of view.

WRITE

Now write your news story about the Galveston Hurricane of 1900.

Make sure your news story

☐ begins with a headline and introduction that will catch the attention of readers.

☐ tells events in the order in which they happened.

☐ includes important facts and key details from the text.

☐ uses linking words to show the sequence of events.

☐ ends with a concluding sentence.

Prepare to Read

GENRE STUDY A **play** is a story that can be performed for an audience.

- Plays list a cast of characters. The cast of characters names each character and may include a brief description of the character's role.

- Authors of plays include stage directions to help set the scene and to develop the characters. Stage directions are set in italics and within parentheses.

- Plays use lines of dialogue to reveal the plot.

SET A PURPOSE **Look at** the illustration on the next page. What can you tell about the main character of this play? What questions do you have about her? Write your ideas below.

**Build Background:
The Story of Atalanta**

CRITICAL VOCABULARY

adoringly

capable

spectators

disbelief

CATCH ME IF YOU CAN

by Carol Schaffner • illustrated by Tim Mack

CHARACTERS

NARRATOR
KING HENRY 12
ATALANTA
TWO MESSENGERS
FIVE YOUNG MEN
YOUNG JOHN
SPECTATORS, *4 to 5*

Atalanta

1 **NARRATOR:** Once upon a time, there lived a princess named Atalanta, who could run as fast as the wind. (*ATALANTA runs on, stops to check wind—sticks finger in mouth, holds it up—then runs in place a bit.*) Not only was she a good runner, she was also bright and clever (*ATALANTA points to brain*) and very handy. Atalanta could fix or build almost anything. (*She takes out small hammer and "fixes" chair.*) Many young men thought she was wonderful and wanted to marry her. (*FIVE YOUNG MEN enter, gaze at her adoringly. She turns her back on them, then looks over her shoulder and waves them away. They exit sadly.*) Atalanta's father, King Henry, thought it was high time for her to get married. (*KING enters.*)

---

adoringly   If you act adoringly, you act with a lot of love and admiration.

2 **KING:** Atalanta, my dear, it's time for you to settle down.

3 **ATALANTA** (*Rolling her eyes*): Oh, Dad, we've had this talk before.

4 **KING:** Yes, I know! And you still haven't listened to me. So I have decided to choose your husband for you.

5 **ATALANTA:** You must be kidding! I haven't decided if I even *want* to get married. And if I do, I'm perfectly capable of choosing my own husband. Besides, you've taught me to think for myself, and what I really want to do right now is go out and see the world!

6 **KING:** Wherever did you get such a silly idea?

7 **ATALANTA:** From you, right after you returned from your tenth trip around the world.

capable   If a person is capable, he or she has the skill or ability to do something.

8 **KING:** Oh, well, that was official kingly business—mostly. And since I am king—and your father—you will do as I say!

9 **ATALANTA:** But, Dad . . .

10 **KING:** No buts! I have thought of the perfect way to choose your husband. I will hold a race, and whoever wins will also win the right to marry you.

11 **ATALANTA** (*As if cooking up an idea*): Whatever you say, Dad, but I get to race, too. If I lose (*Steps toward audience*)—and I don't plan to!—(*Steps back*) I will accept the wishes of the young man who wins the race.

12 **KING:** You've got yourself a deal. (*They shake hands, then walk off together.*)

13 **NARRATOR:** The king was pleased, because not only would he get his daughter married, everyone would get to watch a good race. So messengers were sent throughout the kingdom to announce the race. (*TWO MESSENGERS enter, unroll scrolls.*)

14 **1ST MESSENGER:** Hear ye! Hear ye!

15 **2ND MESSENGER:** His Highness, King Henry, announces a race and invites all young men to participate.

16 **1ST MESSENGER:** The winner wins the right to marry his daughter, totally awesome Princess Atalanta.

17 **2ND MESSENGER:** No kidding? Can we try out too?

18 **1ST MESSENGER:** Why not?

19 **2ND MESSENGER:** Let's get out our sneakers. (*They run off.*)

20 **NARRATOR:** Atalanta, determined to win, got up every morning at dawn to run. (*She runs in.*)

21 **ATALANTA** (*Checking time on her watch*)*:* Whew! All this practice is really improving my time. Well, one more jog around the town . . . (*She runs off.*)

22 **NARRATOR:** As the day of the race grew nearer, young men began to arrive. (*FIVE YOUNG MEN enter.*)

23 **1ST YOUNG MAN:** I am so ready for this race!

24 **2ND YOUNG MAN:** Not as ready as I am!

25 **3RD YOUNG MAN:** I even went out and bought a new pair of running shoes. (*Shows off shoes*)

26 **4TH YOUNG MAN:** Just imagine, after the race I'll be marrying Princess Atalanta.

27 **5TH YOUNG MAN:** Hey, don't count your chickens before they're hatched.

28 **NARRATOR:** Just then Young John walked by. He lived in the town and had seen Atalanta only from a distance, but he knew how bright and interesting she was. (*YOUNG JOHN enters.*)

29 **2ND YOUNG MAN:** Hey, Young John, are you going to try out for the race?

30 **YOUNG JOHN:** I was thinking about it.

31 **1ST YOUNG MAN:** You're going to have to do more than just think about it to beat us.

32 **3RD YOUNG MAN:** So you want a chance to marry Princess Atalanta too?

33 **YOUNG JOHN:** Not really. I just want a chance to talk to her, get to know her.

34 **5TH YOUNG MAN:** Talk to her? What's the deal with that? (*MEN scoff at him.*)

35 **YOUNG JOHN:** I just don't think it's right for Atalanta's father to give her away as a prize. She should get to choose who she wants to marry, or even if she wants to get married at all.

36 **1ST YOUNG MAN:** That's really weird. Let's go, guys.
(*YOUNG MEN exit.*)

37 **NARRATOR:** Each evening, to get in shape for the race, Young John went out for a run. (*He runs around stage*.) Soon he could run as fast as the wind.

38 **YOUNG JOHN** (*Jogging in place*): I think I'm ready! Practice really does make perfect. (*Jogs off*)

39 **NARRATOR:** At last, the day of the race arrived! Trumpets sounded (*MESSENGERS enter and blow fanfare on kazoos*)—O.K., kazoos sounded—and the runners and spectators gathered. (*YOUNG MEN, YOUNG JOHN, SPECTATORS, MESSENGERS, and ATALANTA enter. All runners stretch out. KING HENRY enters.*)

40 **KING:** Welcome, welcome, everyone, on this great day! To the runners, I wish you good luck. And to you, my dear Atalanta, I must say farewell. By tomorrow you will be married!

41 **ATALANTA:** Don't be so sure about that, Dad. (*Steps to audience*) They're going to eat my dust!

42 **KING:** Runners, to the starting line! (*They line up at one side of stage*.) On your mark, get set, go! (*All start running in "slow motion." Spectators do silent, "slow motion" cheering.*)

spectators Spectators are people who watch an event, such as a sports competition.

43 **NARRATOR:** At first, the runners ran as a group, but soon Atalanta pulled ahead. (*She does so.*) Before long, most of the runners fell down, exhausted. (*They do, but not YOUNG JOHN*) Except for one runner—Young John kept right up with Atalanta. (*They are side by side now.*)

44 **ATALANTA:** What do you think you're doing?

45 **YOUNG JOHN:** Keeping up with you!

46 **ATALANTA:** I can see that. I'm impressed. (*They smile at each other.*)

47 **NARRATOR:** Atalanta and Young John crossed the finish line side by side. (*SPECTATORS cheer. ATALANTA and YOUNG JOHN stop running, breathing hard, high-five each other.*)

48 **KING** (*Coming to them*): Who is this young man, Atalanta?

49 **ATALANTA:** Father, this is Young John from our town. (*YOUNG JOHN extends hand to KING; they shake.*)

YOUNG JOHN: Pleased to meet you, Your Highness.

KING: Well, Young John, you didn't exactly win the race, but you came closer than any of the other runners. So I award you the grand prize—the right to marry my daughter. (*ATALANTA frowns.*)

YOUNG JOHN: Thank you very much, sir, but I couldn't possibly marry her unless she wanted to marry me. I really would just like a chance to talk to her and get to know her better. (*KING walks over to SPECTATORS, shaking his head in disbelief.*)

ATALANTA (*Smiling*): I'd love to get to know you better, too, but I should tell you right up front—I'm not sure about the marriage thing. What I really want to do is go out and see the world.

YOUNG JOHN: No kidding! That's exactly what I've been planning to do. What are some places you want to visit? (*They start walking off.*) I've just got to see the Pyramids and the Grand Canyon . . .

NARRATOR: And so Atalanta and Young John spent a lovely afternoon together. By the end of the day, they were good friends. The next day, Young John set off to see the Pyramids, while Atalanta took off for China to see the Great Wall. Perhaps some day they will meet up again, who knows? In any case, we can be sure that they are both living . . .

ALL: Happily ever after!

THE END

disbelief Disbelief is not believing that something is true.

Collaborative Discussion

Look back at what you wrote on page 200. Tell a partner two things you learned about Atalanta. Then work with a group to discuss the questions below. Refer to details and examples in *Catch Me If You Can*. Take notes for your responses. When you speak, use your notes.

1 Review page 204. What is the king's plan for finding a husband for his daughter? How does Atalanta react to the plan?

2 Read page 207. What does Young John think about the king's plan? How is Young John different from the other young men?

3 How is the result of the race unexpected?

Write a New Scene

Catch Me if You Can is a play about Atalanta, a princess who is determined to make her own choices about her life. At the end of the play, Atalanta and Young John go their own ways. But the narrator tells the audience, "Perhaps some day they will meet up again."

Imagine that the two *do* meet again. Write a new scene for the play that builds on the events in *Catch Me if You Can* to tell what happens at a future meeting. Be sure to use elements of drama, such as character tags, setting, and stage directions. Don't forget to use some of the Critical Vocabulary words in your writing.

PLAN

Make notes about Atalanta and Young John. Then make notes predicting what you think might happen when they meet again in the future. Be sure to include the setting for your scene.

WRITE

Now write your new scene about a future meeting between Atalanta and Young John.

✓	Make sure your scene
☐	is written like a scene in a play.
☐	includes stage directions that tell how the characters should act and speak.
☐	builds on the events in *Catch Me if You Can* using a structure that clearly explains the action.
☐	includes the setting.
☐	ends with a conclusion.

Notice & Note
Words of the Wiser

Prepare to Read

GENRE STUDY **Autobiographical fiction** is based on the author's own experiences but may also include made-up events and characters.

- Authors of autobiographical fiction present events in sequential, or chronological, order.

- Autobiographical fiction may include sensory details and figurative language.

- Authors of autobiographical fiction tell the story through first-person point of view.

SET A PURPOSE **Think about** what you know about diaries. What would you like to learn about the diary of the main character? Write your ideas below.

Meet the Author:
Amada Irma Pérez
Meet the Illustrator:
Maya Christina Gonzalez

CRITICAL VOCABULARY

burst

opportunities

immigration

refugees

amazing

My Diary from Here to There

Story
Amada Irma Pérez

Illustrations
Maya Christina Gonzalez

1   **D**ear Diary, I know I should be asleep already, but I just can't sleep. If I don't write this all down I'll burst! Tonight after my brothers—Mario, Víctor, Héctor, Raúl, and Sergio—and I all climbed into bed, I overhead Mamá and Papá whispering. They were talking about leaving our little house in Juárez, Mexico, where we've lived our whole lives, and moving to Los Angeles in the United States. But why? How can I sleep knowing we might leave Mexico forever? I'll have to get to the bottom of this tomorrow.

2   **T**oday at breakfast, Mamá explained everything. She said, "Papá lost his job. There's no work here, no jobs at all. We know moving will be hard, but we want the best for all of you. Try to understand." I thought the boys would be upset, but instead they got really excited about moving to the States.

3   "The big stores in El Paso sell all kinds of toys!"

4   "And they have escalators to ride!"

5   "And the air smells like popcorn, yum!"

6   Am I the only one who is scared of leaving our home, our beautiful country, and all the people we might never see again?

---

burst   If you feel like you will burst, you feel great energy that you want to use up.

7   **M**y best friend Michi and I walked to the park today. We passed Don Nacho's corner store and the women at the *tortilla* shop, their hands blurring like hummingbird wings as they worked the dough over the griddle.

8   At the park we braided each other's hair and promised never to forget each other. We each picked out a smooth, heart-shaped stone to remind us always of our friendship, of the little park, of Don Nacho and the *tortilla* shop. I've known Michi since we were little, and I don't think I'll ever find a friend like her in California.

9   "You're lucky your family will be together over there," Michi said. Her sisters and father work in the U.S. I can't imagine leaving anyone in our family behind.

10 OK, Diary, here's the plan—in two weeks we leave for my grandparents' house in Mexicali, right across the border from Calexico, California. We'll stay with them while Papá goes to Los Angeles to look for work. We can only take what will fit in the old car Papá borrowed—we're selling everything else. Meanwhile, the boys build cardboard box cities and act like nothing bothers them. Mamá and Papá keep talking about all the  opportunities we'll have in California. But what if we're not allowed to speak Spanish? What if I can't learn English? Will I ever see Michi again? What if we never come back?

11 Today while we were packing, Papá pulled me aside. He said, "Amada, m'ija, I can see how worried you've been. Don't be scared. Everything will be all right."

12 "But how do you know? What will happen to us?" I said.

opportunities If you have opportunities, you have chances to make something good happen.

13　　He smiled. "M'ija, I was born in Arizona, in the States. When I was six—not a big kid like you—my Papá and Mamá moved our family back to Mexico. It was a big change, but we got through it. I know you can, too. You are stronger than you think." I hope he's right. I still need to pack my special rock (and you, Diary!). We leave tomorrow!

14　　**O**ur trip was long and hard. At night the desert was so cold we had to huddle together to keep warm. We drove right along the border, across from New Mexico and Arizona. Mexico and the U.S. are two different countries, but they look exactly the same on both sides of the border, with giant saguaros pointing up at the pink-orange sky and enormous clouds. I made a wish on the first star I saw. Soon there were too many stars in the sky to count. Our little house in Juárez already seems so far away.

15　　**W**e arrived in Mexicali late at night and my grandparents Nana and Tata, and all our aunts, uncles and cousins (there must be fifty of them!) welcomed us with a feast of *tamales*, beans, *pan dulce*, and hot chocolate with cinnamon sticks. It's so good to see them all! Everyone gathered around us and told stories late into the night. We played so much that the boys fell asleep before the last blanket was rolled out onto the floor. But, Diary, I can't sleep. I keep thinking about Papá leaving tomorrow.

16   **P**apá left for Los Angeles this morning. Nana comforted
Mamá, saying that Papá is a U.S. citizen, so he won't have a
problem getting our "green cards" from the U.S. government.
Papá told us that we each need a green card to live in the
States, because we weren't born there.

17   I can't believe Papá's gone. Tío Tito keeps trying to make
us laugh instead of cry. Tío Raúl let me wear his special
medalla. And Tío Chato even pulled a silver coin out of my ear.
The boys try to copy his tricks but coins just end up flying
everywhere. They drive me nuts sometimes, but today it feels
good to laugh.

18   **W**e got a letter from Papá today! I'm pasting it into your pages, Diary.

19   My dear family,

I have been picking grapes and strawberries in the fields of Delano, 140 miles north of Los Angeles, saving money and always thinking of you. It is hard, tiring work. There is a man here in the fields named César Chávez, who speaks of unions, strikes, and boycotts. These new words hold the hope of better conditions for us farmworkers.

20   So far, getting your green cards has been difficult, for we are not the only family trying to start a new life here. Please be patient. It won't be long before we are all together again.

Hugs and kisses,
Papá

21   I miss Papá so much—it feels like he left ages ago. It's been tough to stay hopeful. So far we've had to live in three different houses with some of Mamá's sisters. First, the boys broke Tía Tuca's jewelry box and were so noisy she kicked us out. Then, at Nana's house, they kept trying on Tía Nena's high heels and purses. Even Nana herself got mad when they used her pots and pans to make "music." And they keep trying to read what I've written here, and to hide my special rock. Tía Lupe finally took us in, but where will we go if she decides she's had enough of us?

22   FINALLY! Papá sent our green cards—we're going to cross the border at last! He can't come for us but will meet us in Los Angeles.

23   The whole family is making a big farewell dinner for us tonight. Even after all the trouble the boys have caused, I think everyone is sad to see us go. Nana even gave me a new journal to write in for when I finish this one. She said, "Never forget who you are and where you are from. Keep your language and culture alive in your diary and in your heart."

24   We leave this weekend. I'm so excited I can hardly write!

25   My first time writing in the U.S.A.! We're in San Ysidro, California, waiting for the bus to Los Angeles. Crossing the border in Tijuana was crazy. Everyone was pushing and shoving. There were babies crying, and people fighting to be first in line. We held hands the whole way. When we finally got across, Mario had only one shoe on and his hat had fallen off. I counted everyone and I still had five brothers. Whew!

26   Papá is meeting us at the bus station in Los Angeles. It's been so long—I hope he recognizes us!

27   What a long ride! One woman and her children got kicked off the bus when the immigration patrol boarded to check everyone's papers. Mamá held Mario and our green cards close to her heart.

28   Papá was waiting at the station, just like he promised. We all jumped into his arms and laughed and Mamá even cried a little. Papá's hugs felt so much better than when he left us in Mexicali!

29   I wrote to Michi today:

30   Dear Michi,

I have stories for you! Papá found a job in a factory, and we're living in a creaky old house in El Monte, east of Los Angeles. It's not at all like Juárez. Yesterday everything started shaking and a huge roar was all around us—airplanes, right overhead! Sometimes freight trains rumble past our house like little earthquakes.

31   Every day I hold my special rock and I think about home—Mexico—and our walks to the park. Papá says we might go back for the holidays in a year or two. Until then, write me!

Missing you,
Amada Irma

> **Immigration**   Immigration is the process of coming to live in a new country. Immigration workers make sure that people follow the laws about moving.

32 **W**ell, Diary, I finally found a place where I can sit and think and write. It may not be the little park in Juárez, but it's pretty. You know, just because I'm far away from Juárez and Michi and my family in Mexicali, it doesn't mean they're not here with me. They're inside my little rock, they're here in your pages and in the language that I speak, and they're in my memories and my heart. Papá was right. I AM stronger than I think—in Mexico, in the States, anywhere.

33 P.S. I've almost filled this whole journal and can't wait to start my new one. Maybe someday I'll even write a book about our journey!

A Note from the Author

34 **W**hen I was only five years old, my family left Mexico for the United States. That time—when we left Juárez behind, stayed with my Nana in Mexicali, waited breathlessly for my father's letters—was exciting, but also painful. I didn't know then that I, like so many other economic and political refugees, could survive in a completely new place.

35 As a teacher, I have heard many amazing stories from my students about their own journeys from one homeland to another. Some of my former students have devoted their lives to helping new immigrants who have also had to leave the comfort of home and country. They, like me, believe that we strengthen each other by telling these stories. With the love of our families and by writing in our diaries, we find the strength to thrive in our new home. Through our words, we keep our memories and culture alive, in our diaries and in our hearts.

—*Amada Irma Pérez*

refugees   Refugees are people who must leave their countries because of war or other serious problems.

amazing   If something is amazing, it is very surprising and wonderful.

Collaborative Discussion

Look back on what you wrote on page 214. Then work with a group to discuss the questions below. Support your answers with details and examples from *My Diary from Here to There*. Take notes for your responses. When you speak, use your notes.

1 Reread page 217. How are Amada's thoughts about moving different from her brothers'? What do you learn about her from this?

2 Review pages 220–222. What do Amada's relatives do to try to help her family? How were the things they did useful?

3 What helped Amada meet the challenges she faced when she moved to a new country?

Listening Tip

After listening carefully to each speaker, think about the main ideas that person has shared.

Speaking Tip

Have the summarizer review all of the responses to each question before going on to the next one. Ask if everyone in the group agrees.

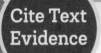
Write a Diary Entry

The author of *My Diary from Here to There* tells the story of her family's journey from their homeland in Mexico to the United States. The story is told from the narrator, Amada's, point of view.

Imagine that you are Amada and that a year has passed since your last diary entry. Write a diary entry in which you tell about your new life in the United States. Don't forget to use some of the Critical Vocabulary words in your writing.

PLAN ....

Make notes about the important events in the text. Then make notes about how you think life might be different for Amanda now.

Now write your diary entry about Amada's life in the United States.

✓ Make sure your diary entry
☐ begins with an introduction.
☐ has a structure that clearly explains events.
☐ connects ideas using words such as *then, because,* and *so.*
☐ uses first-person pronouns such as *I, me, myself,* and *we.*
☐ ends with a concluding sentence.

? **Essential Question**

What does it take to meet a challenge?

Write a Persuasive Letter

PROMPT Think about the challenges the characters faced in *Rent Party Jazz* and *My Diary from Here to There*.

Compare and contrast how each family chose to meet their challenge. Imagine that you know someone who is facing a similar problem. Write a letter to convince the person to try the solution you believe will work. Use evidence from both selections to support your argument.

I will write about _____.

✓ Make sure your letter
☐ states your opinion clearly.
☐ is organized into paragraphs based on clearly stated ideas.
☐ includes text evidence and other details that support your argument.
☐ uses linking words and phrases, such as *because* and *in addition*.
☐ sums up your argument in a conclusion.

What ideas from the selections will help your friend meet his or her challenge? Look back at your notes, and revisit the texts as necessary.

Use the word web to help you plan your argument. Write your argument in the center circle. Then add supporting reasons, facts, and examples in the outer circles.

My Argument: _____

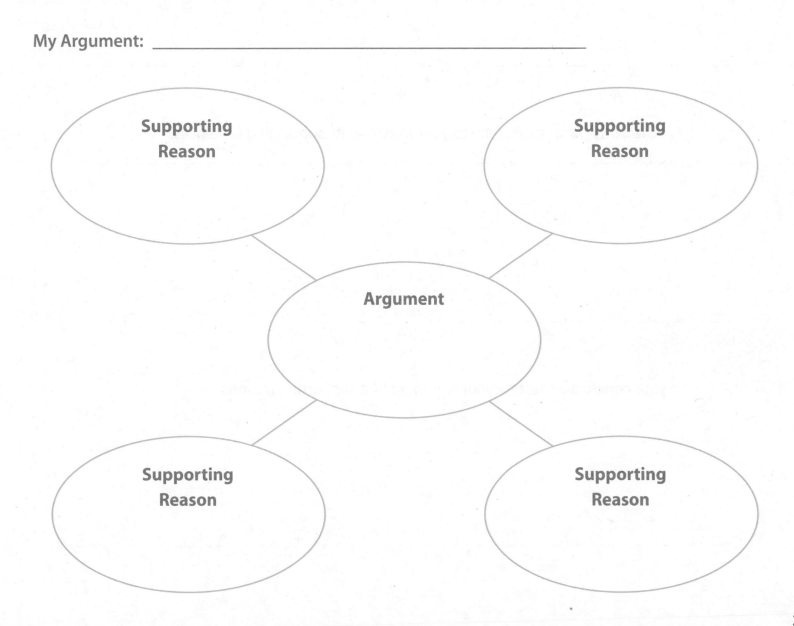

Supporting Reason

Supporting Reason

Argument

Supporting Reason

Supporting Reason

DRAFT .... Write your article.

Write an **introduction** that clearly states your argument.

For the **body paragraph**, refer to your web to write supporting sentences.

In your **conclusion**, restate your argument and supporting reasons.

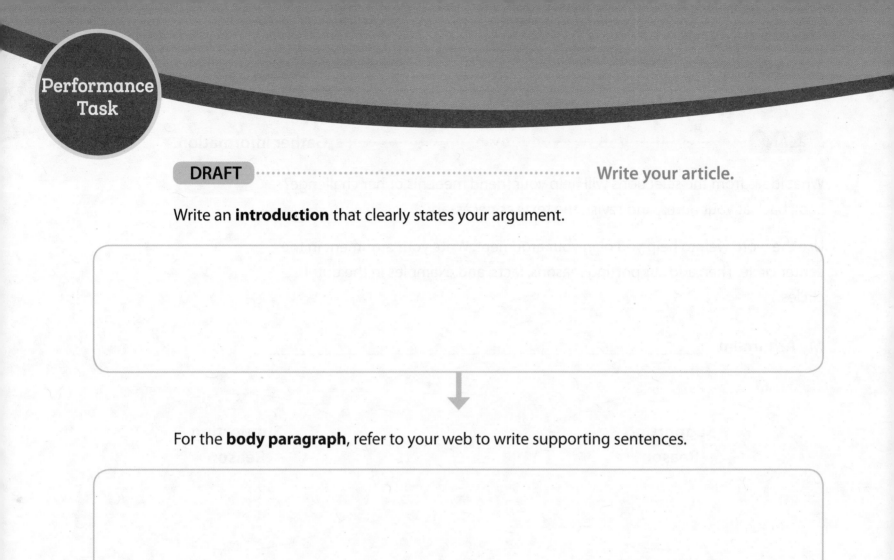

REVISE AND EDIT

Review your draft.

The revision and editing steps give you a chance to look carefully at your draft and make changes. Work with a partner to determine whether you have clearly made your argument and supported it with reasons, facts, and examples. Use these questions to help you evaluate and improve your letter.

PURPOSE/ FOCUS	ORGANIZATION	EVIDENCE	LANGUAGE/ VOCABULARY	CONVENTIONS
☐ Did I state my argument clearly? ☐ Have I written a convincing argument?	☐ Does my letter have a strong introduction? ☐ Have I provided a strong conclusion?	☐ Did I write facts and examples that explain my argument? ☐ Did I include text evidence from my reading?	☐ Did I use linking words and phrases that make my writing flow smoothly?	☐ Is each word spelled correctly? ☐ Have I used capital letters and punctuation marks properly?

PUBLISH

Share your work.

Create a Finished Copy Make a final copy of your letter. Choose a way to share your writing. Consider these options:

1. Add your letter to your writing portfolio so you can see how your writing improves during the year.

2. Scan or create a digital copy of your letter and upload it to your school or class website.

3. Present your letter as a speech to your class. Ask your classmates what they think of your ideas.

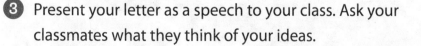

Heroic Feats

"The goal will not be reached if
the right distance is not traveled."

—Tibetan proverb

? Essential Question

What makes someone a hero?

Get Curious

Video

Words About Heroism

The words in the chart will help you talk and write about the selections in this module. Which words about heroism have you seen before? Which words are new to you?

Add to the Vocabulary Network on page 239 by writing synonyms, antonyms, and related words and phrases for each word about heroism.

After you read each selection in this module, come back to the Vocabulary Network and keep building it. Add more ovals if you need to.

WORD	MEANING	CONTEXT SENTENCE
aspire (verb)	When you aspire to do something, you have strong hopes to achieve it.	I aspire to be an author one day.
confidence (noun)	If you have confidence, you have strong and sure feelings about yourself.	Joe has confidence in his ability to do well in the cooking contest.
endeavor (verb)	If you endeavor to do something, you try very hard to do it.	Joon and Juan endeavor to finish the group project before it's due.
fearlessness (noun)	Having fearlessness in a situation means that you are not scared and feel brave.	Climbing the rock wall requires a certain level of fearlessness.

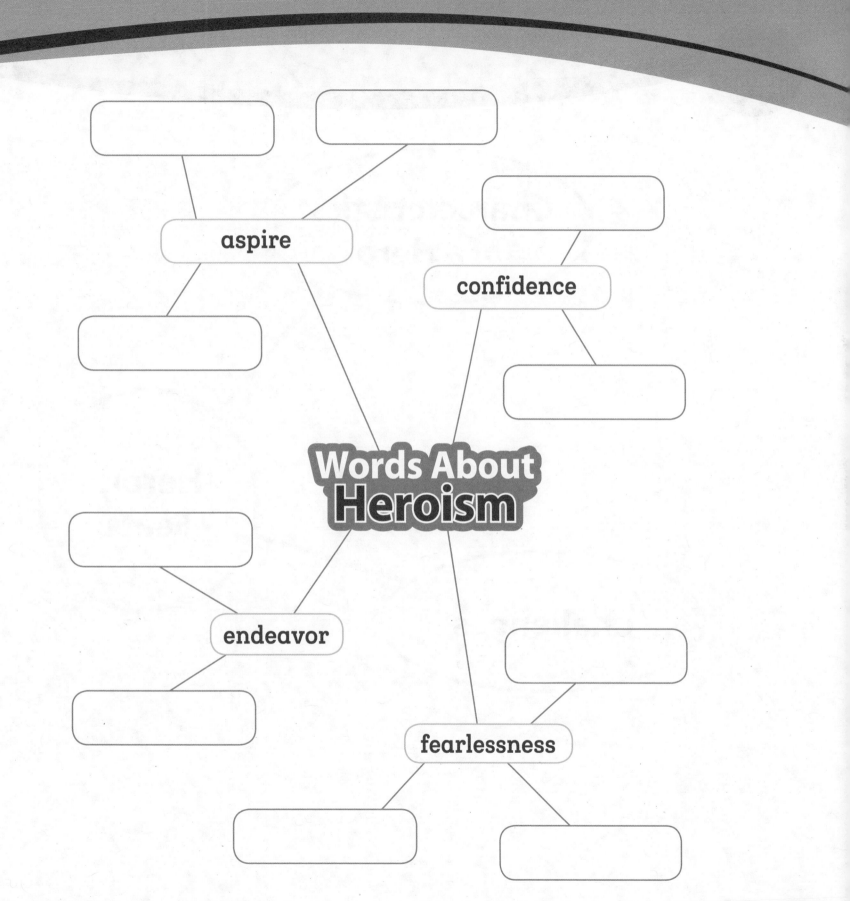

aspire

confidence

endeavor

Words About
Heroism

fearlessness

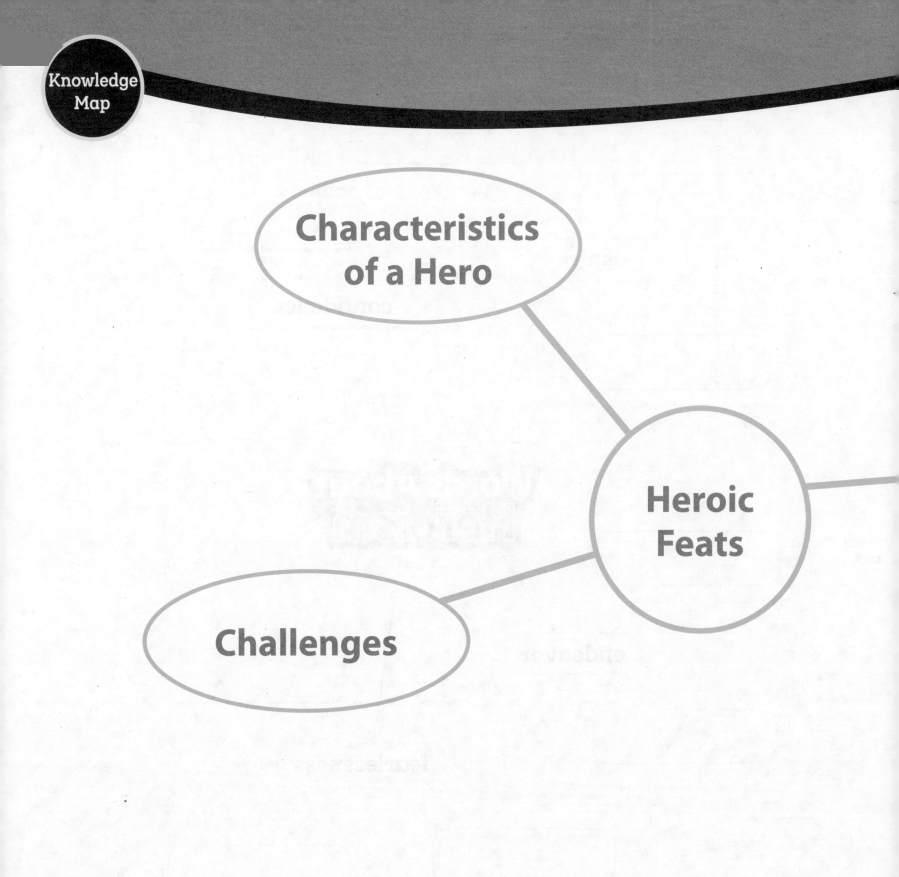

Characteristics
of a Hero

Heroic
Feats

Challenges

Heroes

WHO'S A HERO?

1 Heroes come in many forms. Some heroes are fictional characters. They appear in books or movies. Others are real people. They're folks we see every day. But what exactly makes someone a hero?

A hero is someone who shows COURAGE

2 Many heroes show fearlessness through their brave deeds. In Greek mythology, the hero Hercules has to complete twelve impossible tasks, including killing the Nemean lion and defeating the terrifying Hydra — a monster with nine heads! Hercules courageously completes all his tasks.

3 Real-life heroes are equally courageous. Firefighters don't hesitate to race into burning buildings to rescue people and pets. Airline pilots sometimes land planes in brutal weather. Being brave is part of their work. It's what they do.

A hero is someone who CARES

4 Heroes endeavor to improve the lives of others. Doctors and nurses strive every day to treat people suffering from injury and illness. Volunteers step forward to help people, animals, or the environment.

5 The greatest fictional heroes also care. Think about comic book heroes. They perform all sorts of dazzling feats, but it's *why* they do what they do that really matters. They're heroes because they use their superpowers to help others.

A hero is someone who has CONFIDENCE

6 An ancient Chinese legend tells of a young woman named Hua Mulan who bravely takes her father's place in the army, fighting bravely alongside warriors with much more experience. Her secret is her training. Mulan's father had drilled her in the martial arts, so she is sure of herself when she goes into battle.

7 Confidence is crucial for real-life heroes, too. Police officers train carefully so they know how to react in dangerous situations. Hard work and preparation give everyday people the confidence to respond heroically to challenges.

A hero is someone who is DETERMINED

8 Many athletes are heroes because they inspire us with their hard work and determination. Sports heroes spend years sharpening their skills. They may fail more than they succeed, but they seldom give up.

9 The same is true for many fictional heroes. In *Charlotte's Web*, Charlotte is one determined spider. She works valiantly to rescue Wilbur the pig from an unhappy fate. Against all odds, the gentle spider saves her friend's life.

10 Now that you know what it takes to be a hero, why not aspire to be one yourself? You don't need to slay monsters or break records—just find your own special way to be a hero and help make the world a better place!

Prepare to Read

GENRE STUDY **Fairy tales** are traditional tales that tell stories about magical characters and events.

- Authors of fairy tales tell the story through the plot—the main events of the story. The plot includes a conflict, or problem, and the resolution, or how the problem is solved.
- The characters in fairy tales may include royalty.
- Fairy tales include a theme or lesson learned.

SET A PURPOSE **Think about** what you know about fairy tales. What else would you like to learn about this fairy tale? Write your ideas below.

**Meet the Author:
Christopher Healy**

CRITICAL VOCABULARY

elegant

foreboding

episode

scowled

intimidated

subdued

disheveled

rigid

feisty

sulked

Prince Charming Misplaces His Bride

King Wilberforce

Prince Fre...

Ella

by Christopher Healy
illustrated by Davide Ortu

In the fictional nation of Harmonia, there lives a charming prince named Frederic who has craved a life of adventure ever since he was a boy and met a visiting knight. Frederic's father, King Wilberforce, shields his son from any activity that might cause his son harm. Prince Frederic is not allowed to wrestle, do martial arts, or explore caves. One day, the King comes up with a plan to make Frederic forget his thirst for all things exciting. He arranges for Frederic to train a tiger. (The tiger is toothless and already trained, but Frederic doesn't know that.) Nevertheless, the prince's attempt at taming the "wild" beast goes very, very wrong. The King thinks his plan has worked. And it does, for a while…

2   More than a decade passed before the thought of adventure found its way back into Frederic's mind. It happened on the night of the big palace ball, at which it was hoped that Frederic would find a bride (he never left the palace, so this type of event was the only way for him to meet girls). Among the dozens of elegant women at the ball that night, there was one girl who caught Frederic's attention immediately—and it wasn't just because she was beautiful and elegantly dressed. No, she had something else: a daredevil gleam in her eyes. He'd seen that look only once before—in that old knight all those years ago.

3   Frederic and the mystery girl had the time of their lives dancing together. But at midnight she ran off without a word.

4   "Father, I have to find that girl," insisted Frederic, newly inspired and feeling a bit more like his seven-year-old self again.

5   "Son, you've never been outside the palace gates," the king replied in a foreboding tone. "What if there are *tigers* out there?"

6   Frederic shrank away. That tiger episode had really done a number on him.

elegant   Someone or something that is elegant is stylish and pleasant to look at.
foreboding   If something is described as foreboding, it suggests that something bad is going to happen.
episode   An episode is an event or period of time that is important in some way.

7   But Frederic didn't give up entirely. He instructed his trusted valet, Reginald, to find the mystery woman for him. It turned out that Ella (that was her name) wasn't a noblewoman at all; just a sooty cleaning girl. But her story—the way she mixed it up with a fairy and used magical means to escape her wicked stepfamily—intrigued Frederic (even if he hoped he'd never have to meet any of her relatives).

8   When he told his father he wanted to marry Ella, the king sputtered in surprise. "I thought I'd fixed you, but apparently I didn't," the king scowled. "You don't get it at all, do you? An ill-bred wife would destroy your image more than any scar or broken limb ever would."

9   Up until that point, Frederic had always believed that the king enforced strict rules because he feared for his son's safety. But now he saw that wasn't necessarily the case. So, for the first time, Frederic stood up to his father.

10   "You do not rule me," he stated firmly. "Well, technically you do, being as you're the king. But you do not rule my heart. My heart wants Ella. And if you don't bring her here to be with me, I will go to her. I don't care how dangerous it is out there. I would ride a tiger to get to her if I had to."

11   In truth, Frederic was utterly intimidated by the thought of venturing out into the real world. If his father refused to meet his demands, he had no idea if he would be able to follow through on his threat. Luckily for him, the king was shocked enough to give in.

12   And so, Ella came to live at the palace. She and Frederic were officially engaged to marry, and the tale of the magical way in which the couple met became the talk of the kingdom. Within days, the minstrels had a new hit on their hands, and the tale was told and retold across many realms. But while the popular version of the story ended with a happily-ever-after for Prince Charming and Cinderella, things didn't go as smoothly for the real Frederic and Ella.

---

scowled   If you scowled, you frowned or had an angry look on your face.

intimidated   Someone who is intimidated feels afraid of someone or something.

13   Ironically, it was Ella's bold and venturesome spirit—the very thing that Frederic found so attractive about her—that came between them. Ella's dreadful stepmother had treated her like a prisoner in her own home and forced her to spend nearly every waking hour performing onerous tasks, like scrubbing grout or chipping congealed mayonnaise from between fork tines. While Ella suffered through all this, she dreamed of a more exhilarating life. She fantasized about riding camels across deserts to search ancient temples for magic lamps, or scaling cloud-covered peaks to play games of chance with the rulers of hidden mountain kingdoms. She honestly believed that *anything* could happen in her future.

14 When Ella met Frederic at the ball, it was the climax of a day filled with magic and intrigue, and she assumed it was the beginning of a nonstop, thrill-a-minute existence for her. But life with Frederic was not quite what she'd expected.

15 Frederic tended to sleep in. Sometimes until lunch. And he'd often spend over an hour grooming himself to his father's specifications. By the time Ella finally saw him each day, she would be more than ready for some sort of excitement. But Frederic usually suggested a more subdued activity, like picnicking, listening to music, or quietly admiring some art.

16 Don't get me wrong: Ella enjoyed all those things—for the first few days. But by the fourteenth picnic, she began to fear that those same few activities were all she was ever going to do at the palace. Her unchanging routine made her feel uncomfortably like a prisoner again. So one morning, she decided she would speak frankly with Frederic about what she needed.

17 That morning, as usual, Frederic slept late. When he eventually got up, he spent fifteen minutes (pretty quick for him) browsing a closet filled with ultra-fancy suits, before finally deciding on a crisp white outfit trimmed with gold braiding and tasseled shoulder pads. The five minutes after that were dedicated to straightening his short, light-brown hair. Unfortunately, a few stubborn strands refused to stay in place, and so the prince did what he did whenever he got frustrated:

18 "Reginald!"

19 Within seconds, a tall, slender man with a thin, pointy mustache popped into the prince's bedroom. "Yes, milord?" he asked in a voice stiff enough to match his rigid posture.

> **subdued**   Something that is subdued is quiet and low key.

20   "Good morning, Reginald," Frederic said. "Can you fix my hair?"

21   "Certainly, milord," Reginald said, as he grabbed a silver brush and began using it to tidy the prince's bed head.

22   "Thank you, Reginald," Frederic said. "I'm off to see Ella, and I want to look my best."

23   "Of course, milord."

24   "I think I'm going to have Cook surprise her with breakfast in bed."

25   Reginald paused. "I'm reasonably sure, milord, that the young lady has already eaten breakfast."

26   "Drat," muttered the prince. "So it's happened again. How long ago did she wake up?"

27   "About three hours ago," Reginald replied.

28   "Three hours! But I asked you to wake me when Ella got up."

29   "I'm sorry, milord," Reginald said sympathetically. "You know I'd love to help you. But we're under strict orders from the king: Your beauty sleep is not to be disturbed."

30   Frederic burst from his seat, waving away Reginald's brush. "My father *ordered* you not to wake me? He's still trying to keep me and Ella apart."

31   He rushed to the door of his bedroom, then quickly back to the mirror for one last check of the hair, and then out and down the hall to look for his fiancée.

32   Ella wasn't in her room, so Frederic headed to the gardens. He paused briefly to sniff a rosebush, when he heard the sound of approaching hoofbeats. He looked over his shoulder to see that a large white horse was bearing down on him, tearing through the garden at a fast gallop, leaping over one hedgerow after another. The prince tried to run, but the golden tassels of his jacket caught on the shrub's thorns.

33   Frederic tugged frantically at his stuck sleeve as the horse's rider pulled up on the reins and brought the steed to a halt. From the saddle, Ella looked down at him and laughed. She wore a distinctly unfancy blue dress, and her tied-back hair was disheveled from the ride. Her strong, athletic build and warm, healthy glow were a stark contrast to Frederic's slender frame and sun-deprived complexion. "I hope you haven't been stuck there all morning," she said, only half joking.

disheveled   If something is disheveled, it is not neat or tidy.

34   "No, this just happened," Frederic said, relieved. "I don't suppose you could possibly hop down and lend me a hand?"

35   Ella slid off the saddle, patted her horse's nose, and crouched down to help free the prince's jacket from the thorns. "I told you those tassels would get you into trouble someday," she said.

36   "But they're what all the most fashionable noblemen are wearing these days," Frederic said brightly.

37   He brushed himself off and struck a chest-out, hands-on-hips pose to show off his outfit. He hammed it up to get a laugh out of Ella. It worked.

38   "Very nice," Ella said with a chuckle. "I'd love to see you up on a horse sometime," she hinted, petting her mare's pink nose.

39   "Yes, I'm sure I'd look positively heroic up there," Frederic said. "It's a shame I'm allergic to horsehair." He wasn't allergic; he was afraid of falling off.

40   "A terrible shame," Ella sighed.

41   "I didn't realize you knew how to ride," Frederic said. "Considering the way your stepmother kept you under lock and key, I wouldn't have thought you had much time for equestrian lessons."

42   "I didn't," Ella said. "Charles, your head groom, has been teaching me these past few weeks. I usually practice in the mornings, while you . . . um, while you sleep."

43   Frederic changed the subject: "So, have you heard the song that Pennyfeather wrote about you? That bard of ours certainly has a way with a quill. The song is very popular, I hear. Supposedly, the minstrels are singing it as far as Sylvaria and Sturmhagen. Before you know it, you'll be more famous than me. Or even more famous than Pennyfeather. Though I don't really like the fact that he called you *Cinder*ella. Makes you sound dirty and unkempt."

44 "I don't mind," said Ella. "I *was* dirty and unkempt for years. I was always covered in soot and cinders from cleaning the fireplace, so at least I see where he got the name from."

45 "Speaking of names," said Frederic, "have you noticed that the song refers to me as 'Prince Charming'? My real name's not in there at all. People are going to think I'm the same prince from that Sleeping Beauty song or the Rapunzel one. Here, listen and tell me what you think." He called out to a passing servant, "Excuse me, my good man. Could you please fetch Pennyfeather the Mellifluous for us? Tell him that the prince and Lady Ella would like a command performance of "The Tale of Cinderella."

46 "I'm sorry, milord", the servant replied. "Mr. Pennyfeather is unavailable. He hasn't been seen for days, actually. It's the talk of the palace; we assumed you would have heard by now. No one knows where the royal bard is."

47 "Well, that explains why I haven't been getting my lullaby these past few nights," Frederic said thoughtfully.

48   "Frederic, maybe something awful has happened to Pennyfeather," Ella said, sounding a bit too excited by the prospect. "We should check into it. Come on, let's go. We need to figure out the last person to see him. Let's start by asking at the gate—"

49   "Oh, I'm sure it's nothing so dramatic," Frederic said quickly. The only thing he had a harder time imagining than a crime occurring within the royal palace was himself investigating such a crime. "He's probably just off at a bard convention somewhere, one of those gatherings where they vote on the precise number of feathers a minstrel should have in his cap—that sort of thing. But don't worry, just because Pennyfeather himself isn't here doesn't mean we can't have music. I'll just send for—"

50   "Never mind the song, Frederic," Ella said, taking a deep breath. "Remember how we were just talking about my sheltered childhood?"

51   Frederic nodded.

52   "Now that I'm free, I want to have new experiences. I want to find out what I'm capable of. So, if we're not going to look into Pennyfeather's disappearance, what can we do today?" she asked. "What kind of adventure *can* we have?"

53   "Adventure, right." Frederic pondered his options briefly. "It is a lovely day. Nice and sunny. I'm thinking picnic. "

54   Ella slumped. "Frederic, I need to do something different."

55   Frederic stared at her like a lost baby rabbit.

56   "I hear there's a troupe of traveling acrobats in town," Ella suggested. "Maybe we could get them in here to teach us some tumbling,"

57   "Oh, but I've got that problem with my ankle." He had no problem with his ankle.

58   "How about a treasure hunt?" Ella proposed excitedly. "Some of the kitchen staff were gossiping about a bag of stolen gold that one of your father's old valets hid in the tunnels below the castle. We could try to find it."

59   "Oh, but I can't go below ground level. You know what dampness does to my sinuses." Dampness did nothing to his sinuses.

60   "Can we go boating on the lake?"

61   "I can't swim." This was true.

62   Ella huffed. "Frederic, what *can* we do? I'm sorry if this sounds rude, but I'm bored."

63   "We could have a different *kind* of picnic," Frederic offered hopefully. "We could do breakfast food for lunch. Croissants, poached eggs. How's that for shaking things up?"

64   Ella walked back to her horse and hopped up into the saddle. "Go ahead and order your picnic, Frederic," she said flatly. "I'm going to ride a bit more while you wait."

65   "Okay," Frederic said, and waved to her. "I'll stay right here."

66   "I'm sure you will. You're very good at that," Ella replied. And she rode off.

67   An hour or so later, Frederic sat out on the palace lawn (well, on a carefully unfolded blanket, actually—he didn't want to get grass stains on his white pants), waiting for his lunch and his fiancée to arrive. A servant arrived and set down a tray of breakfast delicacies in front of Frederic. "Milord," the man said, as he bowed and backed away. "There's a message there for you."

68   Frederic saw a folded piece of paper nestled between a bowl of grapefruit slices and a plate of chocolate-chip waffles. He picked up the note, with a sudden sinking feeling about what it might say.

69 *Sweet, good-hearted Frederic,*

70 *I'm terribly sorry to do this to you, and I hope that someday you will understand why I had to leave. You seem very comfortable in your life here at the palace. I can't make you into someone who wants to climb mountains, paddle rushing rivers, and explore ancient ruins. You don't want to do those things, and that's fine. It's just not your cup of tea. Your cup of tea is, well, a cup of tea.*

71 *But I need something more.*

72 *When you mentioned that song about Rapunzel, it got me thinking. The prince in that story tried to rescue Rapunzel, but Rapunzel ended up rescuing HIM.*

73 *Now, THAT girl is an inspiration. So, I'm heading off to find her. I think Rapunzel and I will hit it off. I think she'll make a great partner for hunting down Pennyfeather. And even if we end up finding him at a boring old convention like you say, who knows what kind of adventures will be in store for us along the way?*

74 *Frederic, you are a lovely man and I have nothing but good wishes for you. For what it's worth, that night at the ball really was the most romantic night of my life.*

75 *All the best,*

76 *Ella*

77 Frederic dropped the letter onto his empty plate. *So,* he thought, *the ball was the most romantic night of her life, huh? Well, that's not saying much coming from a girl whose typical nights consisted of scraping dead spiders out of cracks in the floorboards. And look how she signed it. "All the best"? That's how you sign a thank-you note to your dog walker.* Frederic had completely lost his appetite.

78 "Reginald!"

79   "Am I really that boring?"

80   Frederic was back in his room, sitting slumped on the edge of his cashmere-covered bed, while Reginald, rigid as ever, stood next to him, awkwardly patting the prince's head.

81   "There, there, milord," the valet answered. "I don't think the Countess of Bellsworth would call you boring. Do you remember how elated she was when you taught her how to cha-cha? You have many, many admirers, sir."

82   "Yes," Frederic said sorrowfully. "But Ella is apparently not among them."

83   "It seems that Lady Ella simply seeks a different kind of life than that which you can provide for her here at the palace," Reginald said.

84   "Poached eggs! How stupid can I be?" Frederic smacked himself on the forehead.

rigid   Something that is rigid is stiff and does not bend easily.

85 "There will be other women, milord."

86 "I don't want any other women. I want *Ella*. Reginald, what do you think I should do? And be honest with me; don't just tell me what you think my father would want you to say."

87 Reginald considered this request. He'd been caring for Frederic since the prince was a child. And he'd never been more proud of Frederic than when he saw the young man stand up to his overbearing father. Frederic could use someone as feisty and fearless as Ella in his life.

88 "Don't let her get away," Reginald said, dropping his overly stiff posture and speaking in an unusually casual tone.

89 "Wow," Frederic gasped. "Did you just get two inches shorter?"

90 "Never mind me," Reginald said. "Did you hear what I told you? Get a move on! Go after Ella."

91 "But how?" Frederic asked, still bewildered to hear his longtime valet speaking like a regular person.

92 "We'll put you on a horse. Charles can show you the basics. You don't need to be the world's best rider; you just need to be able to get around. Stick to the roads and you'll be fine."

93 "But—"

94 "I know you're scared, Frederic. But here's my advice: Get over it. Ella wants someone as adventurous as she is. A real hero."

95 "Then I've got no hope." Frederic sulked. "I'm a fantastic dresser. My penmanship is top-notch. I'm really good at being a prince, but I'm pretty lousy at being a hero."

96 Reginald looked him in the eye. "There's a bit of courage in you somewhere. Find it. Go catch up with Ella, wherever she is. And just see what happens. She might be impressed enough that you've left the palace."

feisty   Someone who is feisty is bold, energetic, and determined.
sulked   If you sulked, you were crabby because you were annoyed or disappointed about something.

97 "There's no way my father will allow me to do this."

98 "We won't tell him."

99 "He'll notice I'm gone eventually. And when he does, he'll send his men to retrieve me."

100 "Whichever way you go, I'll send them in the opposite direction."

101 "I'm still not sure I should. It's really dangerous out there."

102 "That's your father talking," Reginald said. "Look, if you go on this journey, you're not just doing it for Ella, you're also doing it for that little boy who once wanted to try everything."

103 "You mean my cousin Laurence, who broke his leg trying to fly with those wax wings?"

104 Reginald looked at him soberly. "Frederic, you don't really remember your mother, but I do. And I know what she'd want you to do."

105 Frederic stood up. "Okay, I'll go."

106 "That's the spirit," said Reginald.

107 Frederic marched out of his room. A second later, he marched back in.

108 "I should probably change into something more appropriate for the outdoors," he said.

109 Reginald put his arm around him. "You don't own anything more appropriate for the outdoors," he said with a smile. "Come, let's get you down to the stables."

Collaborative Discussion

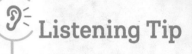

Look back at what you wrote on page 244. Tell a partner two things you observed about this fairy tale. Then work with a group to discuss the questions below. Refer to details and examples in *Prince Charming Misplaces His Bride* to explain your answers.

1 Reread pages 246–248. What do you learn about Frederic from the way he reacts to meeting Ella?

2 Review pages 260–262. How is Reginald's reaction to Ella's disappearance different from what readers might expect?

3 In what ways do Frederic and Ella seem alike? In what ways are they different?

Listening Tip

Look at group members as they speak and notice the facial expressions or gestures they use to help explain their ideas.

Speaking Tip

Make eye contact to help you tell whether others understand your ideas and supported opinions.

Write a Feature Story

PROMPT ···

In *Prince Charming Misplaces His Bride,* you read about Prince Frederic and Ella, two very different characters.

Imagine that you write for the official website of the royal kingdom of Harmonia. You have been assigned to write about Prince Frederic and Ella. Use information from the story to help you write a short feature story about them. Be sure to use some of the Critical Vocabulary words.

PLAN ···

Make notes about details in the text that show what Frederic and Ella are like.

WRITE ....

Now write your feature story about Prince Frederic and Ella.

Make sure your feature story

☐ begins with an attention-grabbing introduction.

☐ compares and contrasts the characters.

☐ describes the characters' actions.

☐ uses description and other details from the story.

☐ ends with a concluding sentence.

myNotes

Notice & Note
3 Big Questions

Prepare to Read

GENRE STUDY **Narrative nonfiction** gives factual information by telling a story about real people, places, and events.

- Narrative nonfiction presents events in sequential, or chronological, order. This helps readers understand what happened and when.
- Social studies texts also include words that are specific to the topic.
- Narrative nonfiction includes visuals, such as photographs or illustrations, maps, and diagrams.

SET A PURPOSE **Look at** the title and image on the next page. What do you think smokejumpers do? What do you want to learn about smokejumpers? Write your ideas below.

CRITICAL VOCABULARY

timid

strenuous

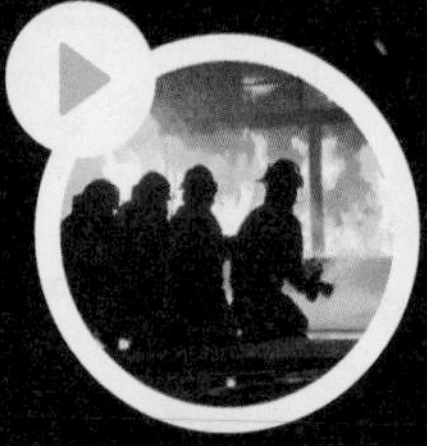

Build Background: Firefighters

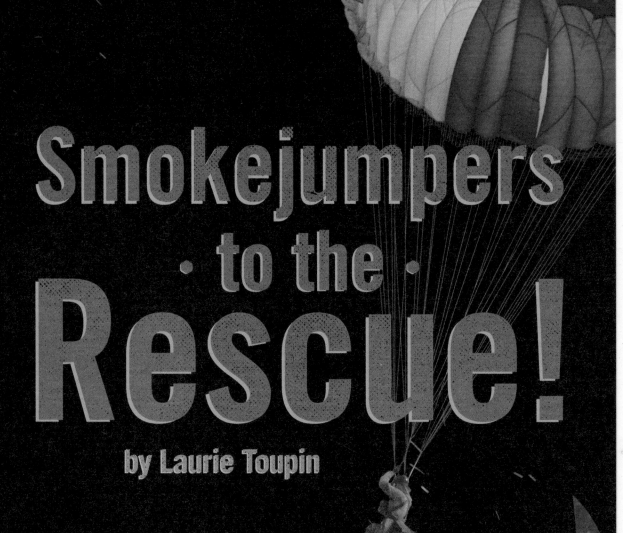

Smokejumpers to the Rescue!

by Laurie Toupin

1   An airplane circles above Dutch Oven Gulch, Idaho, at one hundred miles per hour. A man stands at the open side door of the plane, his hands firmly gripping the sides. His heart races. The plane bounces like a yo-yo in the wind; a fire rages 2,000 feet below. The man waits for his signal.

2   "Get ready . . . Go!" He jumps straight out, gets his body into the right position, then counts: "One thousand one, one thousand two, one thousand three, one thousand four . . . " His parachute opens on "four," pulled by the static line still attached to the plane.

3   Nineteen more jumpers follow, and the plane flies off. Smokejumper Patrick Withen is falling at thirteen feet per second, but he feels as though he is floating. Birds faintly chirp around him; wildfire roars below.

4   Withen lands in a tree outside the burning area. He drops a line, releases his chute, and lowers himself to the ground.

5   All twenty jumpers have landed safely. Now the plane circles back and drops ten boxes, one for each pair of jumpers. The boxes contain everything they need for living and for fighting fire for three days: chain saws, shovels, Pulaskis (part ax and part hoe), first-aid kits, food, and water. If they have to stay longer, more supplies will be dropped in. The jumpers unpack and get to work.

Smokejumpers must parachute into areas that cannot be reached by vehicle.

A trainee adjusts her bag at the U.S. Forest Service Smokejumping Training Center in Missoula, Montana.

Practice, Practice, Practice!

9 Smokejumping is not for the timid. First, would-be smokejumpers must pass a strenuous endurance test. Then begins six weeks of grueling "boot camp": physical endurance training (running, swimming, aerobics, weightlifting, and more) and parachute training (jump skills, landing rolls, and chute packing). "If you don't like making your bed, you won't like packing your parachute," says Withen. It takes an expert thirty-five to forty minutes to properly pack a chute; a beginner might take two days!

6 A smokejumper's most important task is to create a firebreak. That's a stretch of ground in which there's nothing left to burn: no trees, branches, shrubs, or leaf piles. Smokejumpers try to make the fire burn itself out by taking away its fuel.

7 But why not reach the fire from the ground? Why jump into it? "There is a rule that says the closest available resources must respond to a fire. That's often the smokejumpers," says Withen. A fire truck thirty miles away from a wildfire could take an hour or more to reach the blaze. Airplanes are much faster. "Even if we are one hundred miles away, we can be working on that fire within thirty-five minutes," says Withen.

8 There are close to a dozen smokejumping bases throughout the United States. Thanks to the smokejumpers and other dedicated firefighters, many lives and thousands of acres of wild land are saved each year.

> **timid**   If you are timid, you are very careful and often fearful.
> **strenuous**   If an activity is strenuous, it takes great effort or a lot of energy.

Collaborative Discussion

Look back on what you wrote on page 266. Then work with a group to discuss the questions below. Use details and examples from *Smokejumpers to the Rescue!* to support your answers. Take notes for your responses. When you speak, use your notes.

1 Reread page 268. What kinds of feelings do smokejumpers experience when they jump to a wildfire? How do you know?

2 Review pages 268 and 270. What do the smokejumpers' supplies tell you about what they do to fight a fire?

3 What kinds of people make good smokejumpers?

Listening Tip

Give your full attention to each member of your group. Show you are listening by looking at the speaker.

Speaking Tip

As you speak, look at the others in your group. Does anyone look confused? Invite that person to ask you a question!

Write a Job Posting

PROMPT

In *Smokejumpers to the Rescue!* you read about the heroic job done by some special firefighters.

Imagine that you are the leader of a group of smokejumpers and you want to hire someone new to join your team. Write a job posting that will help you find just the right person to become the next smokejumper. Be sure to use some of the Critical Vocabulary words in your writing.

PLAN

Make notes about the problems a smokejumper must solve. Note the characteristics and skills a smokejumper would need to do these tasks.

WRITE

Now write your job posting.

Make sure your job posting

☐ begins with a clear topic sentence focusing on the central idea.

☐ has a structure that clearly explains the ideas.

☐ includes facts and details about characteristics and skills needed for the job.

☐ uses transition words to show connections between ideas.

☐ ends with a concluding sentence.

Prepare to Read

GENRE STUDY *Perseus and the Fall of Medusa* is a Greek myth told in the form of a play. A **myth** is an ancient story that may be about the idea of good and evil. A **play** is a story that can be performed for an audience.

- Plays use of lines of dialogue to reveal the plot.
- Plays use stage directions to help set the scene and to develop the characters. Stage directions are set in italics.
- Characters in myths typically include gods, goddesses, or other beings with superhuman power.

SET A PURPOSE **Think about** what you know about myths. What do you want to learn about some of the mythical characters in this play? Write your ideas below.

CRITICAL VOCABULARY

devised

distress

odyssey

destiny

mortal

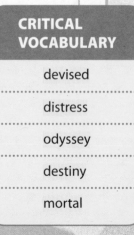

**Build Background:
Heroes in Greek Mythology**

PERSEUS AND THE FALL OF MEDUSA

retold by Claire Daniel * illustrated by Pep Boatella

CAST *of* CHARACTERS

Polydectes
a king

Perseus
son of Danae

Danae
mother of Perseus

Athena
goddess of courage

Zeus
father of all gods

Hermes
god of travel

Medusa
a monster

Andromeda

SCENE I

SETTING: Ancient Greece

Lights up on a large banquet hall where people are standing and chatting. Lights go up on Polydectes, who stands upper stage right.

1 **Polydectes:** (*sweeping his arms toward the door*) Behold my banquet. Everyone is invited, but all know that the price of admission is a gift fit for a king.

2 (*A man bows and presents a golden goblet to the king.*)

3 Yes, a golden goblet is a worthy gift. (*He laughs.*) Yet soon Perseus will come with no gift. He is penniless but loaded with pride, which I intend to use to my good. I have devised a plan to marry his mother, Danae, who so far has refused me. Yes, the trap is set. Soon Danae will be mine. (*He raises his fist to indicate victory.*)

4 (*Perseus enters, holding the hand of his mother.*)

5 **Polydectes:** Ah, Perseus, son of Zeus, and the lovely Danae. What gift do you bring to your king?

6 **Perseus:** My king, you surely know I cannot afford an expensive gift.

7 **Polydectes:** Attention, everyone! This man insults his king by bringing no gift!

8 (*Crowd twitters in disapproval.*) Are you so lazy that you spend your time gazing up at the stars and wishing on them for your fortune? (*Crowd laughs.*)

9 **Perseus:** (*angrily*) I can give you any gift you wish! (*A hush fills the hall.*) Just name it!

10 **Polydectes:** That's quite a claim.

11 **Perseus:** Tell me what you want.

---

devised If you devised a plan, you figured out a way to achieve that plan.

12 **Polydectes:** (*innocently*) If it's not too much trouble . . . I'd really like to have the head of the gorgon, Medusa.

13 **Crowd:** Ooooohhhh!

14 **Perseus:** (*firmly*) No monster will stop me. I will travel the world to get the job done.

15 **Polydectes:** (*takes Danae's hand*) And I will look after your fair mother until you return . . . *if* you return.

16 **Danae:** (*in distress*) Perseus, no! This odyssey will mean certain death!

17 **Polydectes:** Don't worry, Danae. Can't you see that your son has the courage of an army?

18 **Perseus:** (*aside*) What a fool I am! Medusa's face is framed with a hideous mop of snakes. Any man who looks upon her is turned to stone. But if destiny calls me to die, so be it!

Lights dim.

SCENE II

Lights up on Perseus, who stands in Medusa's bedroom. Medusa is sleeping. Snakes from her head hiss at his arrival.

19 (*Enter Zeus, Athena, and Hermes. Perseus kneels to them.*)

20 **Zeus:** Arise, son. (*Perseus rises.*) Your bravery is remarkable, and we have come to help you. Take this, my sword. It cuts through any substance as though it is soft butter.

21 **Athena:** I give you this shield, which acts like a mirror. When you approach Medusa, look into the shield, so her reflection cannot hurt you. Also take this knapsack. The head is harmless inside it.

distress	If you are in distress, you are very worried and upset.
odyssey	An odyssey is a long journey that is exciting and eventful.
destiny	A person's destiny is what will eventually happen in his or her life.

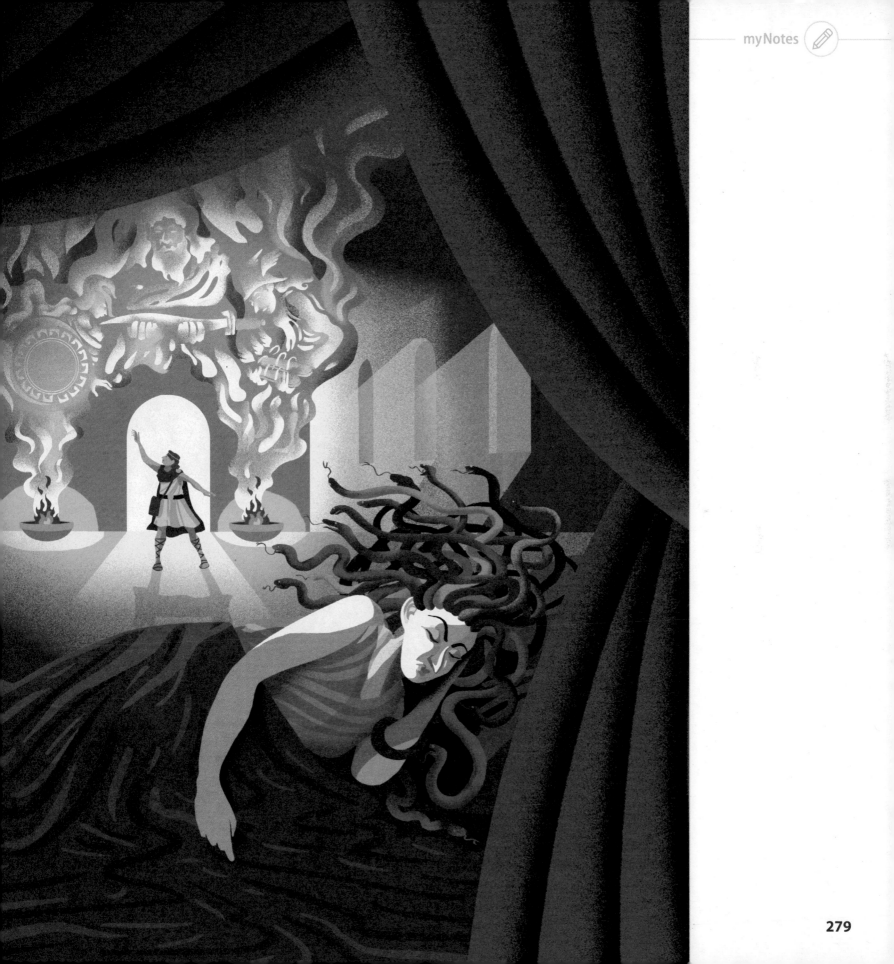

22 **Hermes:** (*handing Perseus sandals with wings*) Take my winged slippers. They will fly you away from all harm.

23 **Perseus:** I promise to bring honor to you all.

24 (*Zeus, Athena, and Hermes exit.*)

25 (*Lights come up on Medusa. Using the reflection from the shield, Perseus approaches Medusa, who awakens.*)

26 **Medusa:** (*hissing*) So you come to harm me. More courageous men than you have fallen to me. (*louder*) Look at me, you coward!

27 **Perseus:** Ah, but that I could look at you, but your looks are deadly to me and any other mortal. You bring death wherever you appear, so it is time for you to meet your end.

> **mortal**   A mortal is a person who lives and dies. In myths, gods are not mortal because they live forever.

28 **Medusa:** And how will you escape? You will not! My sisters will attack you!

29 **Perseus:** Perhaps, but I wear winged slippers that will carry me to the god Zephyr. He will carry me on his soft winds back to my home.

30 (*Medusa moves toward him, the snakes from her head reaching out toward him. Perseus raises his sword.*)

Lights turn to black.

SCENE III

Lights up on Andromeda, who is chained to a rock overlooking the sea. Perseus, holding knapsack and sword, comes down from the sky and stands beside her.

31 **Perseus:** What is your crime, dear lady, that you are chained to this rock?

32 **Andromeda:** My mother angered Poseidon, the god of the sea. He overheard my mother boast that I was more beautiful than his daughter.

33 **Perseus:** And so you are!

34 **Andromeda:** Perhaps, but not for long. Poseidon has set me as bait for the sea monster. I shall be the monster's next meal.

35 (*A breeze moves her hair softly as a whisper, which stirs feelings of love from Perseus.*)

36 **Perseus:** Don't be afraid. The sea monster will eat no more.

37 **Andromeda:** (*pointing to sea*) There, it arises!

38 **Perseus:** Look away from me!

39 (*She does, and Perseus withdraws Medusa's head from the knapsack. The sea monster turns to stone and sinks in the sea. Then Perseus cuts the chain with his sword to free Andromeda.*)

40 **Andromeda:** Kind sir, you have returned a life to me I thought had been stolen.

41 **Perseus:** Give me your hand, then, and I will protect you on your journey through life.

42 **Andromeda:** Who are you, kind sir?

43 **Perseus:** I am Perseus, son of Danae.

44 **Andromeda:** Oh. (*sympathetic*) Then I am sorry, sir, for you.

45 **Perseus:** Why so? I just found you. I'm the luckiest man alive.

46 **Andromeda:** Don't you know what has happened to your mother?

47 **Perseus:** No, how is she?

48 **Andromeda:** She refused to marry Polydectes, so he put her in the dungeon to punish her.

49 **Perseus:** (*angrily*) The king has gone too far! Come, we will reverse this wrong.

Lights dim.

SCENE IV

Lights up at the palace of Polydectes, where Polydectes sits on a throne surrounded by lords, ladies, and guards.

50 (*Enter Perseus and Andromeda.*)

51 **Polydectes:** Perseus, you live to see another day! How very clever you are!

52 **Perseus:** King Polydectes, this is Andromeda. (*Andromeda bows.*)

53   **Polydectes:** Is she the gift you bring? I do need another servant.

54   **Perseus:** Not at all! I've come to claim my mother!

55   **Polydectes:** Very well. (*motions to guard*) Go fetch her! (*pause*) I take it you did not succeed on your odyssey. I knew you to be a failure from the minute I met you. You know now that I will have to banish you from my kingdom . . . or worse.

56   **Perseus:** Whatever pleases the king.

57   (*Guard returns with Danae.*)

58   **Polydectes:** Here she is, safe and sound.

59   **Perseus:** (*loudly*) Mother, Andromeda, and anyone who calls me your friend should look away!

60   (*Danae and Andromeda look away, but everyone else ignores his request. Perseus pulls out Medusa's head from the knapsack, and everyone but Danae and Andromeda turn to stone. Perseus places the head back in the bag.*)

61   **Danae:** Perseus! You have saved us all!

62   **Perseus:** I want you to meet my new wife. Mother, meet Andromeda.

63   (*They all hug.*)

64   **Danae:** My brave son. Great things will come of you. Come, let's leave this horrid place. And let us celebrate your wedding!

Lights dim.

The End

284

Collaborative Discussion

Look back at what you wrote on page 274. Tell a partner two things you learned about myths. Then work with a group to discuss the questions below. Refer to details in *Perseus and the Fall of Medusa* to explain your answers. Take notes for your responses.

1 Reread pages 277–278. What details help you know what Perseus is like?

2 Review pages 278–281. How is Perseus able to conquer Medusa?

3 What is similar about the ways in which Perseus rescues Andromeda and Danae?

Listening Tip

Listen closely to information the speaker shares. Be sure the speaker has finished before you volunteer to share your ideas.

Speaking Tip

Wait for your group's leader to call on you. Then, speak clearly and make eye contact with each member of your group.

Write a Summary

PROMPT

In *Perseus and the Fall of Medusa,* you read a play about a hero who goes on a quest to slay a monster and defeat an evil ruler.

Imagine that your class is putting together a list of action and adventure stories for fourth graders. The list will include plot summaries of these stories. Write a summary of *Perseus and the Fall of Medusa*. Use dramatic, exciting language that will make others want to read the play. Use some of the Critical Vocabulary words in your writing.

PLAN

Make notes about the problem that Perseus faces in the story and how he solves this problem.

WRITE

Now write your plot summary.

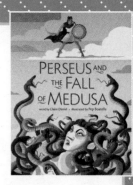

☑ **Make sure your plot summary**
☐ begins by introducing the play, its characters, and its setting.
☐ presents the problem that the main character must solve.
☐ describes events in the order in which they happen.
☐ uses descriptive words and phrases.
☐ provides a concluding sentence.

Notice & Note
3 Big Questions

Prepare to Read

GENRE STUDY **Narrative nonfiction** gives factual information by telling a true story.

- Narrative nonfiction presents events in sequential, or chronological, order.

- Authors of narrative nonfiction may organize their ideas using headings. The headings tell readers what the next section of text will be about.

- Narrative nonfiction includes visuals, such as photographs, illustrations, maps, and diagrams.

SET A PURPOSE **Look at** the picture on the next page. What do you want to learn about the Alamo? Write your ideas below.

▶ Build Background:
The Alamo

CRITICAL VOCABULARY

surrendered

rebellion

furious

tyrant

occasionally

secure

THE BATTLE
OF THE ★ ALAMO

by Amie Jane Leavitt

illustrated by Martin Bustamante

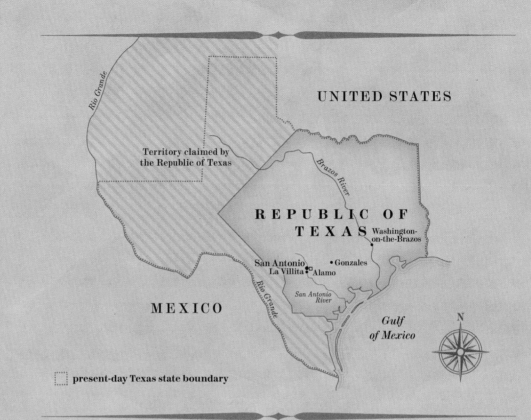

UNITED STATES

Territory claimed by
the Republic of Texas

Rio Grande

Brazos River

REPUBLIC OF
TEXAS

Washington-
on-the-Brazos

San Antonio
La Villita
Alamo

• Gonzales

San Antonio
River

MEXICO

Rio Grande

Gulf
of Mexico

N

☐ present-day Texas state boundary

TAKING SIDES OVER TEXAS

1   It's December 9, 1835. The streets of San Antonio, Texas, are filled with
excitement. After four days of battle, the Mexican leader, General Martin
Perfecto de Cos, has surrendered. The townspeople of San Antonio cheer
when the Mexican Army marches out of the city. Soon the news of the
surrender spreads to other Texas citizens, or Texians.

2   The Mexicans feel ashamed for losing to soldiers they consider to be
backwoods frontiersmen. In 1821, they won their independence from Spain.
And that was against a professionally trained army.

3   If the Texians think they have won the fight, they are wrong. The Mexican
soldiers know they'll be back to reclaim their honor.

surrendered   If you surrendered to an enemy, you gave up and agreed that the other side won.

<4> Across Mexico, many citizens wonder what the fighting is about. After all, Texas is part of Mexico. And even though many Texians are from the United States, most have become Mexican citizens. They always got along with the government. Why are they now fighting against Mexico?

<5> The problems started soon after Antonio López de Santa Anna became president in 1834. After Mexico became free of Spain in 1821, the new leaders wrote a constitution. This set of laws protected the rights of the people and gave them the right to vote. But Santa Anna thought the constitution was making Mexico weak. He decided to make laws of his own. Under these harsher laws, citizens had fewer rights. Most Mexicans went along with the new laws without complaining.

<6> But many Texians felt differently about Santa Anna's laws. They came from the United States. They were used to having more of a say in their government. The Texians worried that giving up a few rights now could mean losing more before long. Some Texian leaders were so angry that they started a rebellion. They wanted Texas to break free of Mexico and become an independent country.

<7> News of the rebellion in Texas made it back to Mexico City. Santa Anna was furious. How dare these rebels try to steal Mexico's land? In late 1835, he sent General Cos to deal with the Texians. The Mexicans and Texians fought many battles. But after this last battle on December 9, the Mexicans were forced out of Texas.

Antonio López de Santa Anna

<8> Now, Mexican citizens all around you are making difficult choices. Many Mexican citizens support Santa Anna. They believe Texas should remain with Mexico. Others are choosing to fight with the Texian rebels.

rebellion   In a rebellion, people defy authority and fight for change in their political system.
furious   Someone who is furious is very, very angry.

★

FIGHTING FOR TEXAS

9   You were born in Louisiana. You came to San Antonio 10 years ago to buy land and became a Mexican citizen. You paid your taxes and obeyed the laws.

10   But you no longer want to be a Mexican citizen. You think Santa Anna's strict laws are unfair, and you've joined with many other Texians in a fight for independence.

11   Since General Cos was defeated, rumors have buzzed around town. Some claim Santa Anna is marching north with an army of thousands.

12   Others say he won't come until spring. Just in case, you send your wife and children to Louisiana, where they'll be safe.

13   Nearly 150 men make up the garrison in San Antonio. Only a few men are trained soldiers. William Travis is one of the leaders. He shares command with Jim Bowie, who is one of your best friends.

14   A few men have joined the garrison from the United States. The other day, famous frontiersman Davy Crockett led a group from Tennessee into town.

15   Early in the morning on February 23, you are standing guard at San Fernando Church. Suddenly, you spot movement on the horizon. Hundreds of soldiers are marching from the south! The rumors were right. You yank the bell's rope. "Santa Anna is coming!" you yell.

16   Townspeople dash through the streets. Many flee the town. Others rush into the Alamo. Church leaders called missionaries lived in the Alamo about 100 years ago. Some buildings in the Alamo don't have roofs, and the tall walls surrounding the buildings are crumbling. But it's still the safest place to go.

17   Once inside the Alamo, you see Almaron Dickinson struggling with the cannons. Nearby, Travis is sending John Smith to the town of Gonzales to round up volunteers to help fight.

18   You rush to Dickinson's side. "Is your family safely inside?" you ask.

19   "Yes, Susanna took baby Angelina into the sacristy," he says. The tiny sacristy is near the chapel. It's probably the safest place in the Alamo.

20   As you work on the cannons, more residents make their way into the Alamo. Some men lead cows into the back pen. Others cart corn into storage rooms. "We could be locked up in here for weeks," you mutter to yourself. "I'm glad we'll have plenty of food to eat."

21   Suddenly, you hear a child's cry for help. You peek through a small window. Eight-year-old Enrique Esparza is standing below you. The Alamo's front gates have already been locked and he can't get in. You lift him through the window. *"Gracias!"* he shouts, as he races to find his father, Gregorio— one of the volunteer fighters.

22   Just then, William Travis approaches the cannons. "Santa Anna is here!" he cries, pointing to the San Fernando Church. The Mexicans have raised a red flag from the bell tower. When Travis sees it, he scowls. "Ha! Santa Anna wants us to surrender, but we're not giving up!" He pounds his fist on a cannon. "Fire it!" he orders. "We'll never surrender to that tyrant!"

tyrant   A tyrant is a powerful person who rules others in a cruel or unreasonable way.

William Travis spots Santa Anna's army.

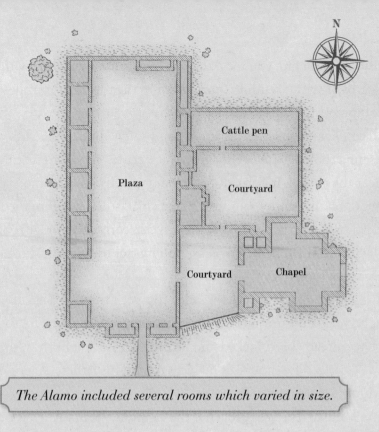

The Alamo included several rooms which varied in size.

23   Dickinson loads the cannon. "Stand clear!" you shout as you pull the cannon's rope tight. Boom! Smoke rings rise as the iron ball soars through the air.

24   The Mexicans respond with cannonfire of their own. They continue firing throughout the evening. Luckily, they're still too far away to do any harm to the walls. Travis orders the cannon crew to fire only occasionally. The cannonballs can't be wasted this early in the attack. He knows they will be needed when the Mexicans move closer to the walls.

25   The next afternoon, Crockett stops you in the plaza. "Jim Bowie is very ill. They think it's typhoid fever," he says.

26   You hurry to Bowie's room. Along the way, a man stops you. "Travis wants us to gather supplies from the shacks in La Villita," he says, pointing to the nearby village. "Will you help us?"

27   You agree to go. You push open the Alamo's heavy wooden gates. Then you sprint 300 yards to La Villita. You must move quickly so the Mexicans don't spot you. You search all the shacks and return with baskets of food, clothing, and blankets.

occasionally   If you do something occasionally, you do it only once in a while.

28   That night, the Mexicans continue shooting cannonballs at the walls. It seems like the explosions are getting louder and louder.

29   The next morning, you're patrolling back in the Alamo. You see a line of Mexicans marching into La Villita. You join a crew atop the wall, aim your rifle, and fire. The Mexican soldiers dive behind the shacks for cover. They return fire, but many have already been hit. The Mexicans retreat, dragging their wounded comrades with them.

30   Later, there is talk that Crockett needs help defending the south wall. You also hear that Travis wants men to burn La Villita so the Mexicans can't use the shacks for protection again. You decide to burn La Villita.

Davy Crockett and other Texians defending the south wall.

31   You meet the other men at the gate. You light a torch and dart toward the small wooden shacks called *jacales*.

32   You touch your torch to the walls of one of the jacales. The shack bursts into flames. You move quickly through the village, lighting each jacale as you go. Soon, La Villita is a fiery scene.

33   Across the river, the Mexicans see the flames. They aim and fire. Luckily, no one is harmed. Your crew is already back inside the Alamo.

The jacales in La Villita quickly burst into flames.

34   On March 1, John Smith returns with 32 men from Gonzales. Travis is grateful they have come. Yet worry shows on his face. He's been sending out messages daily. So far, only the town of Gonzales has responded.

35   Two days later, you walk through the plaza. Smith is leaving to deliver a message to the Texian leaders in the town of Washington-on-the-Brazos. Green Jameson is gathering a crew to repair the crumbling north wall.

36   You follow Jameson to the north wall. It's crumbling from the constant cannon fire. The Mexicans are now only about 250 yards away.

37   You must move quickly to stop the wall from caving in completely. You hammer wood braces and shovel dirt against the stone. After several hours, Jameson tells you to stop. "We've done the best we can for now," he says.

38   The next morning, you visit the sacristy with Gregorio Esparza. His children race to his side. Almaron Dickinson and his wife rock their baby to sleep. You spend the day there with your friends. You're grateful that your family is far away from this place.

39   On the afternoon of March 5, you return to help Jameson secure the north wall. Davy Crockett approaches. "Travis has ordered a meeting in the main plaza," he says.

> **secure**   When you secure an area, you make it safe from being attacked.

40 As you enter the plaza, the bright sun warms your face. Everyone is here—the defenders, the women, and the children. Even Bowie is carried into the plaza on his cot.

41 Travis addresses the group. You can tell by the sad look on his face that he doesn't have good news. "I've sent many letters to the Texian leaders asking for help," he says. "Yesterday, I saw the Mexicans building ladders to climb the walls. I doubt any more volunteers will get here before they attack."

42 You study the faces in the crowd. They're all pale with worry. Everyone knows what a fight without more defenders means. It's impossible for fewer than 200 men to fight off thousands of soldiers.

43 "I will fight to my last breath," Travis continues. He removes his silver sword from the sheath at his side. He uses it to cut a line in the sand. It stretches from one end of the plaza to the other. "Now you must decide. Cross the line if you want to stay and fight for the liberty of Texas."

44 Davy Crockett, Almaron Dickinson, and Gregorio Esparza step across the line. Even Bowie is carried across the line on his cot. Within minutes, all have crossed the line except for you and a Frenchman named Louis Rose. "I can't stay and die here," Rose says. "This is not my war to fight."

Legend says Travis drew a line in the sand with his sword at the final meeting at the Alamo.

45   You think of your own wife and children. You don't want to die, leaving them all alone. What would they do without you? Yet, your friends will need all the help they can get.

46   You're sad at the thought of leaving your friends. But you must do what's best for your family. "I'm sorry, but I must leave too," you say. You glance at the men around you. No one frowns upon you. They respect your decision. Travis thanks you for your service. Crockett and Bowie wish you luck.

47   As you prepare to leave that night, you look back one last time across the Alamo. Davy Crockett and his men are guarding the south wall. William Travis and Almaron Dickinson work on the cannons. Candlelight glows from Jim Bowie's room as he struggles to stay alive one more night. You hear the women in the sacristy softly talking. You believe this is the last time you'll see your friends alive.

48   With this image burned in your memory, you climb over the tall stone wall and race into the darkness. You make it past the Mexican batteries without being detected. As you run northward to freedom, you know you've made it. You will see your family again.

REMEMBER THE ALAMO!

49   By dawn on March 6, the Battle of the Alamo was over. The Mexicans won. As he promised, Santa Anna did not take any prisoners. Every Texian defender inside the Alamo died in the battle. All of the women and children in the Alamo were allowed to leave.

50   The Mexicans tore down the Texians' flag. The Mexican red, white, and green battle flag was put up in its place.

51   Santa Anna wanted to make sure every defender was dead, especially the leaders. He demanded to see the bodies of William Travis, Jim Bowie, and Davy Crockett.

52   The Mexican soldiers searched the defenders' bodies for weapons and valuables. Then they heaped the bodies into a pile and burned them.

53   Texians weren't the only ones to die that day. Hundreds of Mexican soldiers were killed or wounded. Santa Anna would have lost far fewer men if he had waited for the 12-pound cannons to arrive. Many Mexican soldiers and officers lost respect for Santa Anna because of his decision to charge the Alamo before the larger cannons arrived.

54   Santa Anna ordered Alamo survivor Susanna Dickinson to carry a warning to Texian leader Sam Houston. If the other rebels did not surrender, they would share the same fate as their Alamo friends.

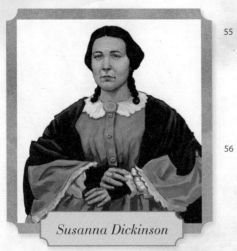

Susanna Dickinson

55 Susanna walked 70 miles east to Gonzales carrying her daughter, Angelina. When she arrived, she gave Houston the message. She also told him what she witnessed at the Alamo,

56 Houston ordered everyone to leave Gonzales. Then he burned the town and marched his army east toward San Jacinto.

57 On April 21, Santa Anna and his men were resting near San Jacinto. Houston attacked and caught Santa Anna by surprise. As Houston's army charged, they shouted the battle cry, "Remember the Alamo!" The battle was over in 18 minutes. This time, the Texians won.

On April 21, 1836, Texians battled Mexican soldiers at the Battle of San Jacinto.

Today, thousands of people visit the Alamo to remember the people who lost thier lives there.

58   Santa Anna was caught during the battle, and he became Houston's prisoner. The Mexican leader begged for his life. Houston let him live, but not without a price. Santa Anna would have to order his armies back to Mexico and stay out of Texas forever. Santa Anna agreed. Texas was finally free.

59   The Republic of Texas remained its own country until 1845. That year, the Texian leaders decided to join the United States. Texas became the 28th state.

60   To this day, the people of Texas still remember the brave defenders of the Alamo. In fact, on the back of the state's seal is a sketch of the old mission's chapel. Above it is written Houston's battle cry from San Jacinto, "Remember the Alamo."

Collaborative Discussion

Look back on what you wrote on page 288. Tell a partner two things you learned from this text. Then work with a group to discuss the questions below. Support your answers with details and examples from *The Battle of the Alamo*. Take notes for your responses. When you speak during discussion, use your notes.

1 Reread pages 290–291. Why are the Texians fighting against Mexico?

2 Review pages 292–293. Who rushes into the Alamo and why?

3 What are some of the hardest decisions that the people inside the Alamo have to make?

Listening Tip

If you can't hear someone in your group easily, ask that person to speak a little louder.

Speaking Tip

Speak using an appropriate volume and pace when giving your opinions and supported ideas.

Write a Journal Entry

PROMPT

In *The Battle of the Alamo,* you learned about events that took place at the Alamo in San Antonio, Texas, in the early 1800s. The author explains the important ideas about this historic event.

Imagine that you were at the Alamo during the battle. Write a journal entry that tells the events of your day. Include your thoughts and feelings, as well as what you are doing. Don't forget to use some of the Critical Vocabulary words in your writing.

PLAN

Summarize the central idea and important details about the events that took place at the Alamo.

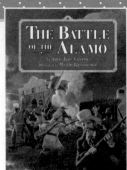

Now write your journal entry describing one day of your life at the Alamo.

✓	**Make sure your journal entry**
☐	introduces a first-person narrator using pronouns such as *I, me, my,* and *myself*.
☐	summarizes the events of the day.
☐	draws on text evidence.
☐	uses sensory words and phrases to describe your experience.
☐	ends with a concluding sentence.

? Essential Question

What makes someone a hero?

Write a Play

PROMPT Think about the types of heroes you read about in this module.

Imagine that you have been chosen to write a play about a hero for a school assembly. Your play will be about a person who has to perform a heroic feat to solve a problem. Look back at *Perseus and the Fall of Medusa* and *Smokejumpers to the Rescue!* for ideas about heroic feats and the character traits of a hero.

I will write a play about _____.

✓ Make sure your play
☐ presents a problem that your hero has to solve.
☐ has a resolution that tells how the problem was solved.
☐ uses stage directions and dialogue to tell the story.
☐ has a theme or lesson that the characters learn.

PLAN .... Organize ideas.

What type of hero will you write about? What is the problem that needs to be solved? Look back at your notes, and revisit the texts as necessary to find the characteristics of heroes.

In the story map below, write the characters, setting, and plot events for your play. Use Critical Vocabulary as appropriate.

My Play: _____

Characters	Setting

Plot Events

DRAFT ·· Write your play.

Write an **introduction** that introduces the main characters of your play and where it takes place.

Write the **events** in the play. Remember, a play tells the story through dialogue. Add stage directions (in parentheses) to show the characters' actions and how they speak.

Write an **ending** for your play that tells how the characters solve the problem.

The revision and editing steps give you a chance to look carefully at your writing and make changes. Work with a partner to determine whether the dialogue and stage directions clearly show what is happening. Use these questions to help you evaluate and improve your play.

PURPOSE/ FOCUS	ORGANIZATION	EVIDENCE	LANGUAGE/ VOCABULARY	CONVENTIONS
☐ Is my play entertaining? ☐ Have I shown how the characters solve a problem?	☐ Does my play have a clear beginning, middle, and ending? ☐ Does my play include a cast of characters, stage directions, and dialogue?	☐ Did I use ideas in the texts to develop characters and events?	☐ Did I use clear action verbs and descriptive language in stage directions?	☐ Have I used correct spelling? ☐ Did I use pronouns correctly? ☐ Did I format my play correctly?

PUBLISH .... Share your work.

Create a Finished Copy Make a final copy of your play. Organize a group of classmates to perform the play. Then choose a way to share your play. Consider these options:

❶ Perform the play for your class as a readers' theater.

❷ Make an audio recording to make a radio play. Have a narrator read stage directions to tell what the characters are doing. Post the recording on a school website to share.

❸ Include your script in a class book of plays or hero stories.

Art Everywhere

"It is the artist who has the courage
to go against the crowd..."

—Henry Miller

? Essential Question

How far can your talents take you?

Get Curious
▶ Video

Words About Artistic Expression

The words in the chart will help you talk and write about the selections in this module. Which words about artistic expression have you seen before? Which words are new to you?

Add to the Vocabulary Network on page 313 by writing synonyms, antonyms, and related words and phrases for each word about artistic expression.

After you read each selection in this module, come back to the Vocabulary Network and keep building it. Add more ovals if you need to.

WORD	MEANING	CONTEXT SENTENCE
sculpture (noun)	A sculpture is something that a person creates by shaping or carving things like clay, stone, or wood.	The clay sculpture that won first prize in the art contest was placed at the front of the classroom.
expressive (adjective)	Someone who is expressive is clearly showing his or her feelings.	The pianist's face was expressive during her solo performance.
inspiration (noun)	If you have an inspiration, you have an excited feeling that gives you new and creative ideas.	One inspiration of mine is my brother, who taught me how to dance.
creativity (noun)	If someone has creativity, they are inventive, especially in the arts.	Aunt Jillian's paintings show her creativity as an artist.

sculpture

expressive

inspiration

creativity

Words About Artistic Expression

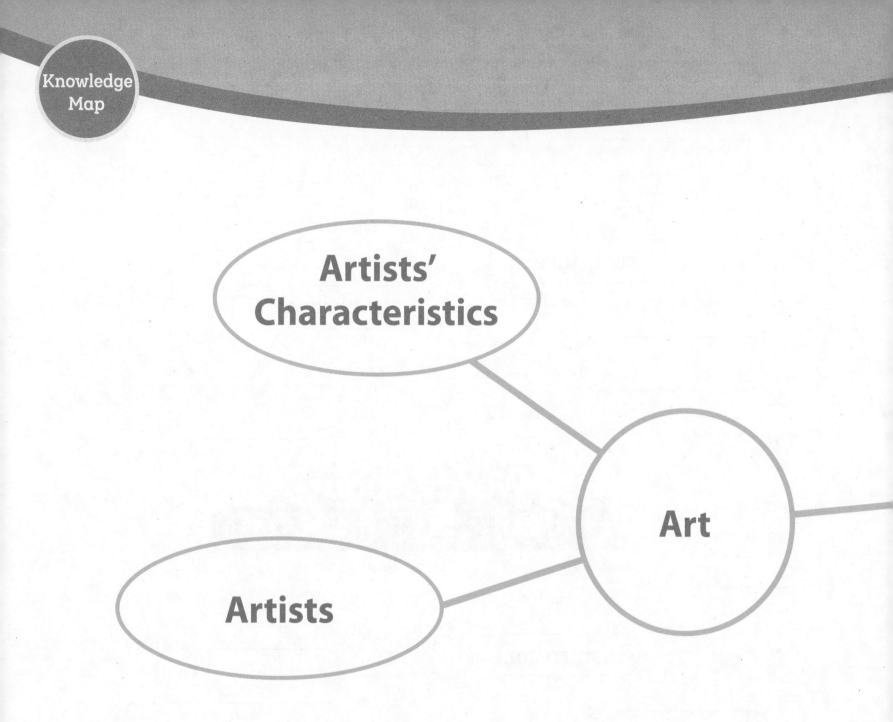

Artists' Characteristics

Art

Artists

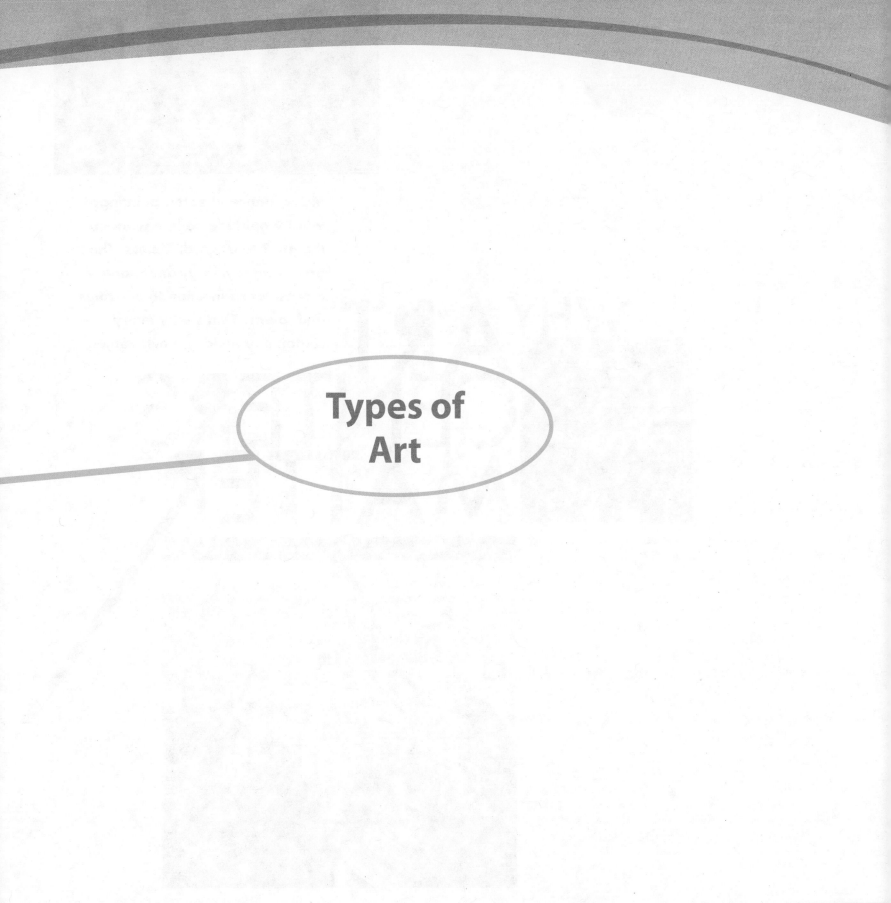

Types of Art

WHY ART CENTERS MATTER

1. Music, dance, theater, paintings—what would life be like without the arts? In a word, lifeless. The arts bring joy, inspiration, and a sense of connection to our cities and towns. That's why every community needs an arts center.

Embracing the Arts

2 An arts center signifies that a community values and supports the arts. A permanent building with galleries to display artworks and stages for performances guarantees that artists will have a place to show and perform their work. It gives them space to be as expressive as they want to be. It also guarantees that people will have a place to experience art of many kinds, including paintings, plays, music, and dance.

Sparking Creativity

3 An arts center also brings people in the community together. It can offer art, music, dance, and theater classes to adults and young people who want to express their own creativity. It can host gatherings for local residents to meet and talk with artists. It can display the work of community members, including students. Its outdoor space can feature not only sculptures, murals, and performance stages but also seating areas and picnic tables, encouraging people to gather.

A Smart Investment

4 It's not inexpensive to build an arts center. However, the payoff can be tremendous. Not only does an arts center enrich the lives of artists and the community, but it also helps nearby businesses. Residents and tourists who visit the arts center are also likely to spend money at nearby restaurants, shops, hotels, and attractions. That boosts the local economy.

5 What's the downside of an arts center? That's easy: There is none! Supporting artists and helping people experience the joy of art are advantages for every community.

Notice & Note
Quoted Words

Prepare to Read

GENRE STUDY   A **biography** is the story of a real person's life written by someone other than that person.

- Authors of biographies present events in sequential, or chronological, order.

- Authors of biographies may use literary language and devices to present major events in a person's life.

- Biographies include third-person pronouns such as *he, she, him, her, his, hers, they, them,* and *their.*

SET A PURPOSE   **Think about** the title and the genre of this text. What do you know about the subject of this biography? What do you want to know? Write your ideas below.

Meet the Authors:
Kathleen Krull and Paul Brewer
Meet the Illustrator:
Stacy Innerst

CRITICAL VOCABULARY

dignified
stunned
polished
regretted
hilarious
observant
flattered
trampled

THE BEATLES WERE FAB

(and They Were Funny)

BY **KATHLEEN KRULL** & **PAUL BREWER**

ILLUSTRATED BY **STACY INNERST**

1   Music was everywhere in Liverpool, where

John Lennon,
Paul McCartney,
George Harrison,
and **Ringo Starr**

grew up. Life wasn't easy in that scruffy city in northern England in the 1940s and '50s, but music made things better. John played guitar and harmonica. Paul started out playing trumpet, but traded it for guitar. George had a guitar, too—and could play circles around John and Paul. Ringo was the best drummer in Liverpool.

2   From the time they got together as lads until they became superstars, the Fab Four made music, made history, and made people laugh.

PENNY LANE
18

3 **John, Paul, George, and Ringo always had fun together, even when they were trying to name their band.**

The Blackjacks
the QUARRY MEN
JOHNNY AND THE MOONDOGS
The NERK TWINS
THE BEATALS
The Silver BEETLES
THE Silver BEATLES
the RAINBOWS
Long John Silver
and the Pieces of Eight
LONG JOHN AND THE BEETLES
The Beetles
THE
BEATLES

4 **In 1960, they finally decided to call themselves the Beatles. The name made them laugh—and it stuck.**

5   In their early days, the Beatles performed for hours and hours in hundreds and hundreds of shows around England and Germany. It was exhausting and paid next to nothing. Anxious to have a record of their very own, the Beatles were afraid the band was going nowhere. They used silliness to help keep their spirits up. John would shout, "Where are we going, lads?"

6   "To the top, Johnny!"

7   "And where is that?"

8   "The toppermost of the poppermost!" the others would yell—and they went on with the show.

9   When they got a new producer in 1962, the Beatles
tried hard to make a good impression, but it wasn't easy.
During a recording session, the producer listed the many
things he didn't like about the music, then said politely,
"Let me know if there's anything *you* don't like."

10   A painful silence. George tried to lighten the mood.
"Well, for a start, I don't like your tie." The producer
laughed, but he still had the Beatles sing their song
seventeen times in a row. It was midnight before he
thought it sounded right.

11   The lads had their first record: "Love Me Do,"
a song Paul had written four years earlier, when
he was sixteen.

12   **O**nce the bouncy tune got on the radio, people started listening. Months later, the Beatles' second record, "Please Please Me," hit number one on the charts in England. The band began appearing on English TV, singing, joking, shaking their mop-top hair, and having a blast. The songs were fantastic, but the lads themselves were so cool, so funny, so fab—short for fabulous—that reporters started calling them the Fab Four.

13   The first Beatles fan club started with thirty-five members and grew to forty thousand within a year. Fans sent their heroes love letters, stuffed animals, and their favorite English candy—squishy jelly babies.

14   It was the birth of something new: Beatlemania. No one had seen or heard a band quite like the Beatles before. Fans followed them everywhere. The lads became clever at escaping crowds, although sometimes they needed help. Once a police officer slung Ringo over his shoulder to get him to safety.

15   The fans wanted more, so John and Paul wrote songs as fast as they could, meeting over tea and corn flakes. As certain words popped up in hit after hit, they began to consider them lucky: *me, please, love,* and especially *you.*

16   When they wrote "She Loves You," Paul's father begged them to change its *"yeah, yeah, yeah"* line to a more proper *"yes, yes, yes,"* but Paul laughed the idea off with a *"no, no, no."* *"Yeah, yeah, yeah"* was soon heard around the world, and "She Loves You" became the first Beatles record to sell a million copies.

17   The Beatles were no longer playing in small seedy clubs. They were even invited to perform for a formal audience that included the British royal family. How should they act? Could the Fab Four still be silly in front of royalty?

18   Before "Twist and Shout," their final song, John invited the main-floor audience to clap along. Then he peered up at the **dignified** royal family in the box seats. "And the rest of you, if you just rattle your jewelry." Everyone giggled—even the Queen Mother.

19   **F**ame came upon them so quickly that the Beatles still couldn't believe it when they heard themselves on the radio. Whenever a Beatles song was scheduled to air, they would stop whatever they were doing, even driving, to listen to the radio with delight.

20   One night in 1964, their manager burst into their hotel rooms at three a.m., waving a telegram from New York in their sleepy faces. Their newest song, "I Want to Hold Your Hand," had hit number one in America. The lads stayed awake for hours, **stunned** that Beatlemania had crossed the Atlantic Ocean.

21   But John still had to joke. He liked to call the song "I Want to Hold Your Nose."

dignified   If you are dignified, you act in a way that is formal, calm, and proper.
stunned   If you are stunned, you are shocked or amazed by something.

327

22 The next month the Fab Four flew to New York, arriving at
John F. Kennedy Airport to the sound of three thousand fans
singing, *"We love you, Beatles, oh, yes, we do!"* Two days after
crossing the Atlantic, they made their first American TV
appearance on *The Ed Sullivan Show*. By then the Beatles had
played together more than a thousand times. Their
performance was as polished as could be, and this turned out
to be the most-watched TV show in history.

polished   A performance that is polished is given with great
skill and no mistakes.

23   **E**ven when the massive audience in America made them nervous, the Beatles didn't show it. All the screaming of the fans was music to their ears—a sign that everyone was having a good time. George said, "We like screams, so scream louder and louder."

24   They were now big stars riding around together in limousines, yet the Beatles had as much silly fun as they'd had as boys in Liverpool.

25   Paul said, "There were just four of us in the back of that car, laughing hysterically." Laughter was their way of dealing with their sudden fame. They joked about everything, but they soon regretted joking about their favorite candy. Soft English jelly babies couldn't be bought in America, so fans started stocking up on jellybeans. They threw jellybeans at the stage during concerts as a way to show their love. Ouch! Jellybeans were much harder than squishy jelly babies. John had an idea: Just eat them.

> **regretted**   If you regretted something, you felt sorry about it and wished you hadn't done it.

26   The Beatlemania roller coaster reached dizzying heights during the 1964 tour. Fans screamed in the Hollywood Bowl, an outdoor stage under the stars; in Denver's Red Rocks Amphitheatre, the music echoing off cliffs of red and orange; in Philadelphia's Convention Hall, in a city filled with history; at the Indiana State Fair, amid the sound and smell of farm animals; and in nineteen more cities from San Francisco to New York.

27   Beatlemania was so intense that the screaming of the fans often drowned out the songs. The lads found it hilarious that the less their music could be heard, the more popular they became and the more money they were paid. Anything they touched went on sale to fans—even the hotel sheets they slept on were cut into tiny squares and sold as souvenirs.

28   Excited fans didn't just miss hearing the music. Sometimes people were so starstruck they didn't hear anything the Beatles said at all. John once tested this by telling a distracted restaurant waiter, "I'd like a steak, medium, and two elephants came and a policeman bit my head off, and a cup of tea, please."

29   Reporters interviewed the band constantly. The Fab Four often thought the questions were silly—and they loved to give silly answers.

hilarious   If something is hilarious, it is very funny.

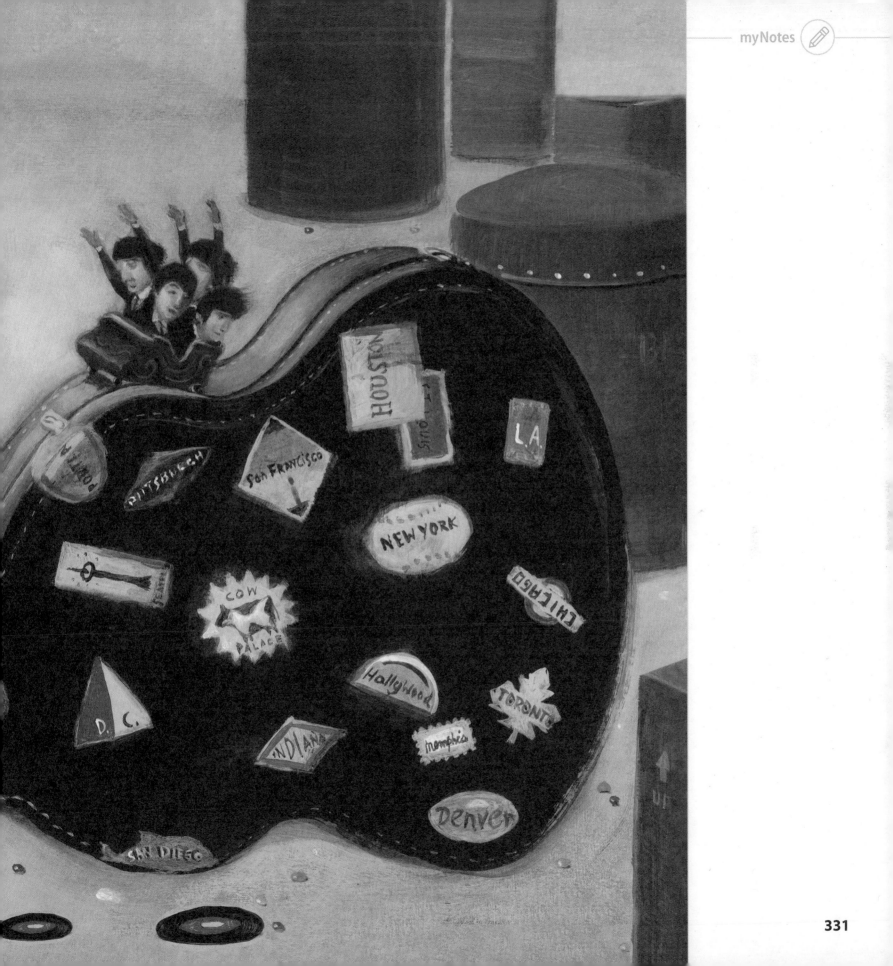

30 **E**very fan has a favorite Beatle. John was often called the smart one.

31 Q: Which one are you?
John: Eric.

32 Q: Some people think your haircuts are un-American.
John: Well, it was very observant of them, because we aren't American, actually.

33 Q: How do you find all this business of having screaming girls following you all over the place?
George: Well, we feel flattered . . .
John: . . . and flattened.

34 Q: Do you go to the barber at all?
Paul: Just to keep it trimmed. But sometimes we do it ourselves, you know.
John: With our feet.

observant   If you are observant, you see or notice more details than other people.
flattered   If you are flattered by something, it made you feel honored or special.

35   **Baby-faced Paul was the cute Beatle.**

36   Q: What is your favorite sport?

Paul: Sleeping.

37   Q: Is your hair real?

Paul: Is yours??

38   Q: You Beatles have conquered five continents. What do you want to do next?

Paul: Conquer six.

39   Q: Will you ever stop being Beatles?

Paul: We are the Beatles. That's what we are.

40 **Younger and a bit shyer, George was sometimes the quiet Beatle.**

41 Q: What do you call your hairstyle?
George: Arthur.

42 Q: What do you do when you're cooped up in a hotel room?
George: We ice-skate.

43 Q: If one of you stopped being a Beatle, what do you think you'd do?
George: I think I'd train elephants in the zoo.

44 Q: What do you do with all the money that you make?
George: I'm going to change all mine into cents, fill up a room, and dive in it.

45 **Nothing rattled Ringo, even rude questions about his large nose.**

46 Q: What do you think of Beethoven?
Ringo: Great. Especially his poems.

47 Q: How many of you are bald, that you have to wear those wigs?
Ringo: All of us.

THE BEATLES

48 Q: How did you find America?
Ringo: We went to Greenland and made a left turn.

49   The Beatles' 1965 American tour opened with the biggest live concert in history so far. A happy crowd of 55,600 fans welcomed them to Shea Stadium in New York. The band's helicopter landed nearby as they watched thousands of flashbulbs light up the sky.

50   This was surely the "toppermost!" And yet, with the wall of screams, nothing else could be heard—not the music, and not even the jets taking off from two nearby airports. This struck the Beatles as so ridiculous that they could do nothing but laugh. But they soon stopped joking, worried about the crowd getting out of control.

51   Later, a reporter asked, "Where would you like to go that you haven't gone yet?"

52   John said, "Home."

53 **F**our years after "Love Me Do," Beatlemania had driven fans wild all over the world. But the Fab Four were forgetting how to laugh. Concerts had bigger problems than jellybeans flying through the air. Now the lads were in danger of being **trampled** by excited fans.

54   At the same time, as they wrote songs that dug deeper into the meaning of life and love, their music was becoming too complicated to perform live.

55   During their last major concert, at Candlestick Park in San Francisco, the fans huddled together on a chilly night. No one quite realized it, but Beatlemania was coming to an end.

trampled   If something is trampled, it is stepped on and damaged or crushed.

56 But it was far from the end of the Beatles and their fun-filled romp. The band retreated to the recording studio, where they could hear the music again and continue to make each other laugh.

57 Nothing was quite the same after Beatlemania. Other British bands became popular, but the witty wordplay of the Fab Four put them in a class of their own. They were trendsetters; everyone wanted haircuts like theirs, and everyone wanted to dress like they did. But most important, they're considered by many to be the greatest rock-and-roll band of all time. Constantly adapting their own music in an extraordinary display of styles and subjects, the Beatles changed music forever.

58 **John, Paul, George,** and **Ringo** recorded more than two hundred songs together. For decades after, their music would inspire people to sing along, dance, love, remember, cry, think, imagine—and laugh.

Collaborative Discussion

Look back on what you wrote on page 318. Tell a partner two things you learned from this text. Then work with a group to discuss the questions below. Refer to details and examples in *The Beatles Were Fab (and They Were Funny)* to explain your answers.

1 Reread page 322. What do you learn about John, Paul, George, and Ringo from the names they thought of for their band?

> They like funny names

2 Review page 330. What kinds of things were surprising to the Beatles as they became famous?

> That they were a great band together

3 How did the Beatles' lives change as they became more famous?

> There song were more serious or less funny

Listening Tip

Listen to what each person in your group has to say so you don't repeat what someone else has already shared. Think of a new idea to share.

Speaking Tip

Stick to the topic! Keep your comments focused on the questions and on the ideas your classmates present.

Write a Book Review

PROMPT

In *The Beatles Were Fab (and They Were Funny)*, you learned how the Beatles went from being a little-known group in England to the most famous band in the world. The author used evidence to support the opinions in the text.

Imagine that you are a book critic and that the newspaper you work for has asked you to write a review of *The Beatles Were Fab (and They Were Funny)*. Write a review that gives your opinion of the book. Use information in the text to support your ideas. Don't forget to use some of the Critical Vocabulary words in your writing.

PLAN

Make notes about ideas, words, and features of the text that support your opinion of the book.

Now write your book review.

✓ Make sure your book review

- ☐ clearly states your opinion of the book.

- ☐ gives reasons for your opinion.

- ☐ uses specific evidence from the text to support your reasons.

- ☐ links your opinion and reasons using words and phrases, such as *because, in order to,* and *in addition.*

- ☐ sums up your opinion at the end.

Prepare to View

GENRE STUDY **Informational videos** present facts and information about a topic in visual and audio form.

- Real people and places in the video help viewers understand the topic.
- Informational videos include words that may be specific to a topic.
- Producers of videos may include sound effects or music to make the video more interesting for viewers.

SET A PURPOSE **As you watch,** think about the subject of the video. What do people in the video say to help you understand more about historical photography? Write your ideas below.

Build Background: Photography

CRITICAL VOCABULARY

curator

foreground

background

How Can Photos Take Us Back in Time?

from *The Metropolitan Museum of Art #metkids*

As you watch *How Can Photos Take Us Back in Time?*, think about the conversational format and how it might help the viewer understand how to analyze historical photographs. How does the conversation help you understand the photographs in the video? Do Kira and the museum curator help make the topic interesting? Why or why not? Take notes in the space below.

Listen for the Critical Vocabulary words *curator*, *foreground*, and *background* for clues to the meaning of each word. Take notes in the space below about how the words were used.

curator   A curator is the person who is in charge of the works of art or objects in a museum.

foreground   The foreground of a picture or photograph is the area that is closest to the viewer.

background   The background of a picture or photograph contains things that are not as noticeable or important as the main objects or people in the photograph or picture.

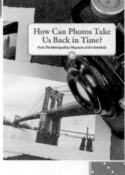

Collaborative Discussion

Look back at what you wrote on page 342. Tell a partner something you learned about historical photography. Then work with a group to discuss the questions below. Refer to details and examples from *How Can Photos Take Us Back in Time?* to support your ideas. During the discussion, listen actively by paying attention to the speaker.

1 What is Kira trying to understand about the photographs?

2 Why do you think photographer Berenice Abbott took the photograph of the Brooklyn Bridge?

3 What is one reason why people study historical photographs?

Listening Tip

Make connections! Listen to each speaker's ideas and think about how you can link them to your own ideas.

Speaking Tip

Build on others' ideas. Explain clearly how your ideas connect to what another speaker has said.

Write a Pamphlet

PROMPT ....

In *How Can Photos Take Us Back in Time?*, you watched and learned about two photographs of the Brooklyn Bridge.

Imagine that you work at the Metropolitan Museum of Art where these photographs are kept. Write a pamphlet that describes the two photographs and what they tell about the Brooklyn Bridge and the times in which the photos were taken. Don't forget to use some of the Critical Vocabulary words in your writing.

PLAN ....

Make a list of ways that the two photographs are alike. Make a separate list of how they are different.

WRITE

Now write your pamphlet to describe the photographs.

✓ Make sure your pamphlet

☐ begins with an introduction to the topic.

☐ describes similarities and differences between the photographs.

☐ includes details from the video.

☐ uses words and phrases such as *also, in addition, but,* and *however.*

☐ ends with a concluding sentence.

Prepare to Read

GENRE STUDY **Informational texts** give facts and examples about a topic.

- Authors of informational texts may organize their ideas by central ideas supported by key details.
- Informational texts include text features, such as bold print, captions, key words, and italics.
- Social studies texts also include words that are specific to the topic. These are words that name things or ideas.

SET A PURPOSE **Think about** the different dance styles you know. Look through the photographs in this selection. What about these dance styles would you like to know more about? Write your ideas below.

Build Background:
Dance

CRITICAL VOCABULARY

rhythmic

distinctive

highlight

horizontal

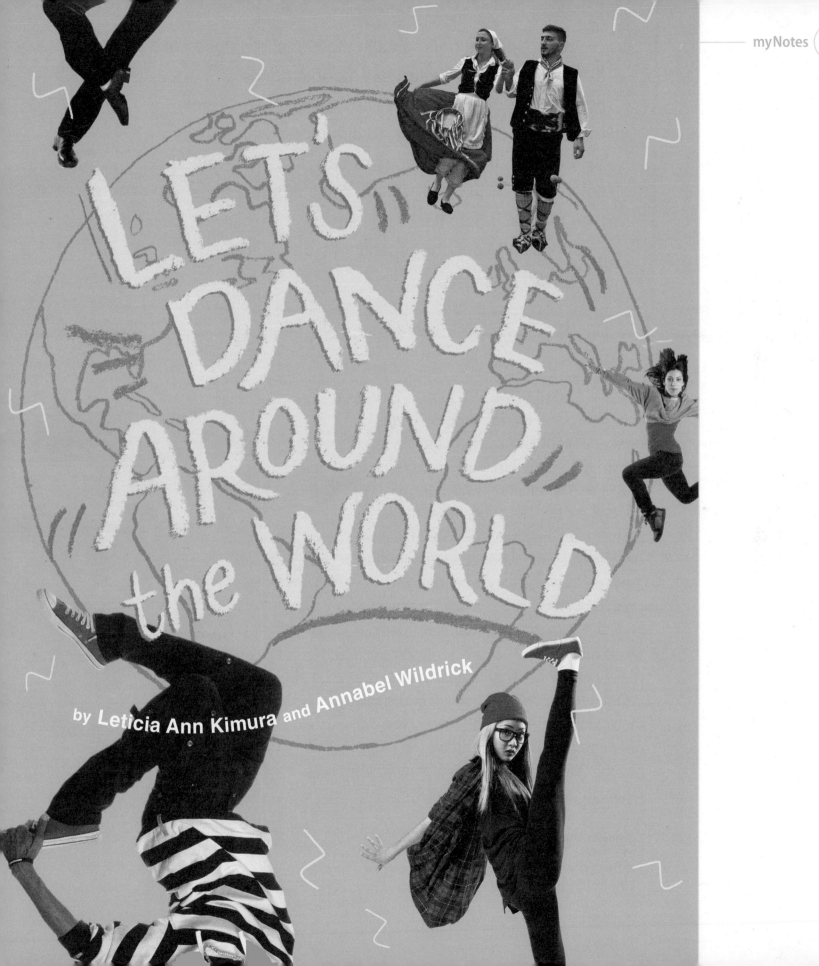

LET'S DANCE AROUND the WORLD

by Leticia Ann Kimura and Annabel Wildrick

1   From glittering ballrooms in big cities to patches of dirt under a starry desert sky, people dance everywhere on our planet. They dance for different reasons, in different ways, to different rhythms. They dance when they are happy or sad, to call for rain, to celebrate a birth. Everywhere, people dance because they just can't help it.

2   So kick off your shoes, and let's dance around the world.

Tap Dance

3   Let's start at home with tap . . . Have you ever heard the sound made by a tap dancer's feet? An American dance, tap is known for the rhythmic heel-toe steps made by the dancers, who wear special shoes. Tap shoes have metal plates at the heel and toe, which make a distinctive sound when the dancers "tap" them on the floor. Tap was originally danced with no music at all. Over the years, however, tap has been danced to many types of music.

4   Savion Glover is an amazing tap dancer. He performed in his first Broadway musical when he was 12. Savion has changed the way people tap—he has brought the rhythms of hip-hop and other music to the tap-dancing stage.

rhythmic   If something is rhythmic, it has a pattern of sounds, movements, or beats that repeat.

distinctive   If something is distinctive, it stands out in a way that makes it different or unusual.

"Break Dance"

5 Speaking of hip-hop . . . If you were to ask five people to tell you what hip-hop is, you'd probably get five different answers. Hip-hop is a way of life that includes the dance style known as breaking, or break dancing. In the 1970s, when rap music was new, hip-hop and breaking were just getting started. Break dancing is usually performed in public places, like city sidewalks. It is highly athletic and involves fast jumps, drops, spins, and robotic freezes. Break dancers can even be seen spinning on their heads!

6   Tap and break dancing are typically done by individuals performing for an audience. Folk dancing, on the other hand, is usually performed by people dancing for themselves. When they dance, most folk dancers wear special clothes, costumes that represent their culture.

7   One of the best-known folk dances in Italy is called the tarantella. A legend about the dance says that people bitten by tarantula spiders danced fast and wildly to try to sweat the poison out of their bodies.

Tarantella

Japanese Folk Dance

8   In Japan, folk dances are often performed at cultural festivals. Japanese folk dancers are known for their slow, graceful movements, dancing with bent knees and bodies low to the ground. They use objects such as umbrellas, swords, and fans to highlight their delicate movements.

9   Traditionally a man's dance, the English morris dance today is performed by both men and women. Dancers hit sticks together and wave handkerchiefs while they hold their bodies straight upright. Bells worn around the dancers' legs jingle, adding to the rhythm.

Los Viejitos

10   In Mexico, there are many popular folk dances. The dance called *los viejitos* (vyay-HEE-tos), which means "the little old men," is meant to help people stay young and active as they get older. Dancers wear masks and hold canes to make themselves look like old men. They start off slowly, then speed up, dancing with lots of energy.

highlight   When you highlight something, you call attention to it.

Limbo

11   The limbo is a competitive dance that originally came from West Africa. The limbo dancer must bend back while dancing under a horizontal pole. If the dancer is successful in passing under the pole without touching it or falling over, the pole is lowered and the dancer tries again. The dancer who goes the lowest is the winner.

12   Brazilian *capoeira* (cap-oh-AY-ruh) blends martial arts and dance. Capoeira dancers perform acrobatic movements like jumps, kicks, flips, handstands, and headstands as they move together in a fake battle.

13   These are just a few of the hundreds of dances around the world. What kind of dancing do you do?

horizontal   If something is horizontal, it is level with the ground.

Collaborative Discussion

Look back at what you wrote on page 348. Tell a partner two things you learned about dance from this text. Then work with a group to discuss the questions below. Refer to details and examples in *Let's Dance Around the World* to explain your answers.

1 Reread pages 350–351. What makes tap dancing different from other types of dance?

2 Review page 353. How do dancers perform the folk dance *los viejitos?*

3 Why is *Let's Dance Around the World* a good title for this selection?

Listening Tip

Keep your mind on what each person is saying. Listen for central ideas and key details. Take notes to help you remember.

Speaking Tip

Try summarizing what another group member has said before adding your own thoughts.

Write a Blog Post

PROMPT

In *Let's Dance Around the World*, you read about many different dance styles and the parts of the world where they are popular.

Imagine that you have a blog where you share ideas about the performing arts. Write a blog post that compares and contrasts two of the dance styles in the text. Add a drawing or diagram to show your ideas. Don't forget to use some of the Critical Vocabulary words in your writing.

PLAN

Make notes about the features of each style of dance. Write how each dance style is similar and how they are different.

WRITE

Now write your blog post that compares and contrasts the chosen dance styles.

Make sure your blog post

☐ introduces the topic.

☐ uses facts and details from the text to describe each dance style.

☐ compares and contrasts the styles of dance.

☐ includes drawings, diagrams, or other visual elements that help readers better understand the information.

☐ ends with a concluding sentence.

Prepare to Read

GENRE STUDY   **Poetry** uses the sounds and rhythms of words to show images and express feelings.

- Poems may be written in one of several styles, such as lyric, acrostic, concrete, or narrative.

- Poets often use figurative language, such as similes and metaphors.

- Poets might organize a poem into stanzas—a series of lines grouped together. Each stanza builds upon what is described in the previous stanza.

SET A PURPOSE   **Think about** the title and genre of this text. What forms of poetry have you read before? What forms do you think you will read? Write your ideas below.

**Build Background:
Poetic Forms**

CRITICAL VOCABULARY

necessary

unsurpassed

stir

extraordinarily

cruising

plunges

THE ART OF
POETRY

—— ILLUSTRATED BY MARINA SEOANE ——

Necessary Gardens

Libraries
Are
Necessary
Gardens,
Unsurpassed
At
Growing
Excitement.

—J. Patrick Lewis

necessary   If something is necessary, it is needed and you can't do without it.
unsurpassed   If something is unsurpassed, there is nothing that is better.

Eating Alphabet Soup

1   My advice to the Tablespoon Slurper:
Beware what you do with that scoop!
        The Capitals, sir,
        Can cause quite a stir
In a bowlful of Alphabet Soup.

2   While K, Z, and B do the backstroke
Across this hot, steamy lagoon,
        The fun-loving Vowels
        May want tiny towels
To dry themselves off on the spoon.

3   But when Letters go swimming together
In sentences, nothing can beat
        The pleasure of reading
        The food that you're eating!
So dive in and—*bon appétit!*

        – *J. Patrick Lewis*

stir   If you cause a stir, you create a strong feeling, such as excitement or shock.

The Big-Word Girl

1　Of all the clever girls I know,
　　　Elaine's the one who counts,
　　But what she counts are syllables
　　　In words I can't pronounce,

2　I took her to a horror show—
　　　(Godzilla Meets Tooth Fairy)—
　　But she could not unglue her eyes
　　　From Webster's Dictionary.

3　She put her trembling hand in mine
　　　(Godzilla smashed the floor!),
　　For she had come across a word
　　　She'd never seen before!

4　But when the lights came on, Elaine
　　　Was sound asleep and snoring.
　　I woke her up. She yawned and said,
　　　"How Uncustomarily,

Extraordinarily,

Incomprehensibly

BORING!"

— *J. Patrick Lewis*

extraordinarily　If something is done extraordinarily, it is very unusual or remarkable in some way.

365

bal on

by Bob Raczka

When
it first slipped out
of my hand, I was sad
to see my balloon floating
away, but as it rose higher
in the sky, I imagined it landing in some faraway yard,
where a kid like me would
find it and wonder how
far the balloon had
flown and who
held it
last,
and that thought made me smile.

The Arrow and the Song

1   I shot an arrow into the air,
    It fell to earth, I knew not where;
    For, so swiftly it flew, the sight
    Could not follow it in its flight.

2   I breathed a song into the air,
    It fell to earth, I knew not where;
    For who has sight so keen and strong,
    That it can follow the flight of song?

3   Long, long afterward, in an oak
    I found the arrow, still unbroke;
    And the song, from beginning to end,
    I found again in the heart of a friend.

—*Henry Wadsworth Longfellow*

Better Fun

1   cruising this river
      on a rubber boat
      at full speed

2   bumping our way
      to the base of
      the thundering falls

3   to end up completely
      slapped and drenched
      by the cool river water

4   beats by far
      any amusement park
      attraction

cruising   If you are cruising, you are traveling in a boat for fun.

Mejor diversión

1   recorrer este río
en un gomón
a toda velocidad

2   acercarse a tumbos
hasta quedar en la base
del trueno de la cascada

3   para acabar completamente
cacheteados y empapados
por el agua fría del río

4   supera de veras en mucho
cualquier atracción
de un parque de diversión

–Francisco X. Alarcón

Quiet Water

1 water before
it plunges down
a waterfall

2 is as still
as a mirror
facing the sky

Agua quieta

1 el agua
antes de caer
en catarata

2 es tan quieta
como espejo
de cara al cielo

— Francisco X. Alarcón

plunges   If something plunges into something, it falls or is thrown in that direction.

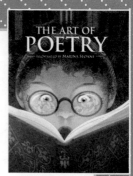

Collaborative Discussion

Look back on what you wrote on page 358. Tell a partner two things you found interesting about the poetry. Then work with a group to discuss the questions below. Find support for your ideas in *The Art of Poetry*. Take notes for your responses. When you speak, use your notes.

1 Reread the poem "The Big-Word Girl" on page 365. What are some of the ways that Elaine is unusual?

> she read a dictionary instead of watching the show.

Listening Tip

If you hear something that you do not understand, try to learn more. Ask the speaker a question about it to make his or her ideas clearer.

2 Review the poem "Better Fun" on page 368. What images do the author's words create in your mind?

> going down a river in a rubber boat in cool water.

Speaking Tip

When you finish speaking, invite the other group members to ask you questions about what you said.

3 Which poem made you think of something in a new way? Explain.

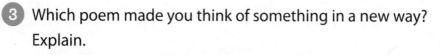
> Quiet water made me image the water how the water is,

Write an Opinion Paragraph

PROMPT

In *The Art of Poetry*, you read poems that used figurative language, sensory words, and rhythm to express ideas.

Imagine that you have been asked to write about your favorite poem for a literature blog. Write an opinion paragraph about the poem that you think makes the best use of word choice, rhyme, and rhythm. Support your opinion with specific details from the poems. Be sure to use some of the Critical Vocabulary words in your writing.

PLAN

Write the name of the poem you think is best. Then, make notes about the poet's word choice, rhyme, and rhythm.

WRITE

Now write your opinion paragraph about the poem you selected.

✓ **Make sure your opinion paragraph**

- ☐ clearly states your opinion of the poem.

- ☐ provides reasons for your opinion.

- ☐ includes specific examples of figurative language and other elements of poetry.

- ☐ uses linking words to connect ideas.

- ☐ provides a concluding sentence.

? **Essential Question**

How far can your talents take you?

Write an Argument

PROMPT Think about what you learned about the different types of art and artistic expression in this module.

Imagine that your school orchestra wants to take a school trip to hear the local professional orchestra. You have been asked to write an argument saying why the trip will be good for the school orchestra. Use evidence from the selections about why art and music are important to support your argument.

I will write about _____.

✓ Make sure your argument
☐ states your argument clearly in the introduction.
☐ is organized into paragraphs that give reasons that support your argument.
☐ includes text evidence and other details.
☐ uses linking words and phrases, such as *because, for instance*, and *in addition*.
☐ sums up your argument in a conclusion.

What ideas will support your argument? Look back at your notes and revisit the texts to find details that show why hearing the local orchestra is important.

In the chart below, write your argument. Then write your reasons to support your argument. Use Critical Vocabulary where appropriate.

My argument statement: _____

Argument

Reason	Reason	Reason

DRAFT ·· Write your argument.

Write an **introduction** that grabs your readers' attention and clearly states your argument.

For each **body paragraph**, write a topic sentence that states one reason for your argument. Add supporting sentences from your chart to explain each reason.

Write a **conclusion** that restates your argument.

The revision and editing steps give you a chance to look carefully at your draft and make changes. Work with a partner to determine whether you have supported your argument clearly. Use these questions to help you evaluate and improve your article.

✓ PURPOSE/ FOCUS	ORGANIZATION	EVIDENCE	LANGUAGE/ VOCABULARY	CONVENTIONS
☐ Have I clearly stated my argument? ☐ Have I stayed on topic?	☐ Does my argument have a clear introduction? ☐ Does each body paragraph focus on one reason that supports my argument?	☐ Have I supported each of my reasons with facts and details? ☐ Are all of the facts and details I chose clearly related to the argument?	☐ Did I use linking words and phrases to show how the facts, reasons, and opinion are related?	☐ Did I indent each new paragraph? ☐ Have I used verb tenses correctly?

PUBLISH ································· Share your work.

Create a Finished Copy Make a final copy of your argument. Consider these options to share your writing:

1 E-mail your argument to your principal.

2 Have a class panel discussion about the importance of local orchestras. Read your argument aloud as part of the discussion.

3 Record yourself reading your argument aloud. Post the audio file on your class website or on your family's social media page.

Glossary

This glossary contains meanings and pronunciations for some of the words in this book. The Full Pronunciation Key shows how to pronounce each consonant and vowel in a special spelling. At the bottom of the glossary pages is a shortened form of the full key.

Full Pronunciation Key

CONSONANT SOUNDS

b	**b**i**b**, ca**bb**age	s	mi**ss**, **s**au**c**e,
ch	**ch**ur**ch**, sti**tch**		**sc**ene, **s**ee
d	**d**ee**d**, mail**ed**,	sh	di**sh**, **sh**ip, **s**ugar,
	pu**dd**le		ti**ss**ue
f	**f**ast, **f**i**f**e, o**ff**,	t	**t**igh**t**, stop**p**ed
	phrase, rou**gh**	th	ba**th**, **th**in
g	**g**a**g**, **g**et, fin**g**er	*th*	ba**th**e, **th**is
h	**h**at, **wh**o	v	ca**v**e, **v**al**v**e, **v**ine
hw	**wh**ich, **wh**ere	w	**w**ith, **w**olf
j	**j**u**dg**e, **g**em	y	**y**es, **y**olk, on**i**on
k	**c**at, **k**i**ck**, s**ch**ool	z	ro**s**e, si**z**e,
kw	**ch**oir, **qu**ick		**x**ylophone, **z**ebra
l	**l**id, need**le**, ta**ll**	zh	gara**g**e, plea**s**ure,
m	a**m**, **m**an, du**mb**		vi**s**ion
n	**n**o, sudd**en**		
ng	thi**ng**, i**n**k		
p	**p**o**p**, ha**pp**y		
r	**r**oar, **rh**yme		

VOWEL SOUNDS

ă	p**a**t, l**au**gh	o͝o	f**u**ll, b**oo**k, w**o**lf
ā	**a**pe, **ai**d, p**ay**	o͞o	b**oo**t, r**u**de, fr**ui**t,
â	**ai**r, c**a**re, w**ea**r		fl**ew**
ä	f**a**ther, k**oa**la, y**a**rd	ŭ	c**u**t, fl**oo**d, r**ou**gh,
ĕ	p**e**t, pl**ea**sure, **a**ny		s**o**me
ē	b**e**, b**ee**, **ea**sy,	û	c**i**rcle, f**u**r, h**ea**rd,
	p**ia**no		t**e**rm, t**u**rn, **u**rge,
ĭ	**i**f, p**i**t, b**u**sy		w**o**rd
ī	r**i**de, b**y**, p**ie**, h**igh**	yo͞o	c**u**re
î	d**ea**r, d**ee**r, f**ie**rce,	yo͞o	ab**u**se, **u**se
	m**e**re	ə	**a**go, sil**e**nt, penc**i**l,
ŏ	h**o**rrible, p**o**t		l**e**mon, circ**u**s
ō	g**o**, r**o**w, t**oe**,		
	th**ough**		
ô	**a**ll, c**au**ght, f**o**r,		
	p**aw**		
oi	b**oy**, n**oi**se, **oi**l		
ou	c**ow**, **ou**t		

STRESS MARKS

Primary Stress ´: biology [bī•ŏl´•ə•jē]

Secondary Stress ´: biological [bī´•ə•lŏj´•ĭ•kəl]

A

absurd (əb'·**sûrd'**) *adj.* If something is absurd, you think it is silly or ridiculous. My dogs looked absurd dressed in clothes and glasses.

accepted (ăk·**sĕp'**·tĭd) *v.* If you have accepted a situation, you understand that it can't be changed. Although I was disappointed at first, I have now accepted that my family is moving to another state.

adapt (ə·**dăpt'**) *v.* If you adapt to something, you figure out how to deal with it. You can adapt to cold weather conditions by wearing a heavy coat and hat.

adoringly (ə·**dôr'**·ĭng·lē) *adv.* If you act adoringly, you act with a lot of love and admiration. My mother makes me feel special when I catch her smiling adoringly at me.

amazing (ə·**mā'**·zĭng) *adj.* If something is amazing, it is very surprising and wonderful. The beauty of the stars in the night sky was absolutely amazing!

ancient (**ān'**·shənt) *adj.* If something is ancient, it is very, very old. The pyramid known as El Castillo is located in the ancient city of Chichen Itza, Mexico.

aroma (ə·**rō'**·mə) *n.* An aroma is a strong, pleasant smell. The aroma of freshly-baked cookies filled the kitchen.

aspire (ə·**spīr'**) *v.* When you aspire to do something, you have strong hopes to achieve it. I aspire to be an author one day.

auction (**ôk'**·shən) *n.* An auction is an event where items are sold to the person who offers the most money. You can purchase just about anything at an auction as long as you are the highest bidder.

awkward (**ôk'**·wərd) *adj.* In an awkward situation, things feel tense and uncomfortable. Learning how to walk put the baby giraffe in some awkward positions.

B

background (**băk'**·ground') *n.* The background of a picture or photograph contains things that are not as noticeable or important as the main objects or people in the photograph or picture. The mountains created a perfect background for a family photograph.

brimming (**brĭm'**·ĭng) *v.* If something is brimming, it is full and about to overflow. My mom likes to relax with a cup that is brimming with hot coffee.

burst (bûrst) *v.* If you feel like you will burst, you feel great energy that you want to use up. We felt like we were going to burst with excitement on the first snow day of the year.

---

o͞o b**oo**t / ou **ou**t / ŭ c**u**t / û f**u**r / hw **wh**ich / th **th**in / *th* **th**is / zh vi**si**on / ə **a**go, sil**e**nt, penc**i**l, lem**o**n, circ**u**s

C

capable (**kā′**·pə·bəl) *adj*. If a person is capable, he or she has the skill or ability to do something. My little sister is capable of putting on her own shoes.

> ### Word Origins
> **capable** The word *capable* is from the Latin word *capere* meaning "take or hold."

cautiously (**kô′**·shəs·lē) *adv*. If you do something cautiously, you do it very carefully. Joe cautiously walked on the log to get to the other side of the stream.

chorus (**kôr′**·əs) *n*. The chorus of a song is the part that is repeated after each verse. During choir practice, our instructor asked us to sing the chorus several times.

clumsy (**klŭm′**·zē) *adj*. If an action is clumsy, it happens in a careless way. Lincoln was clumsy when he knocked over his cup of coffee on his desk.

comfort (**kŭm′**·fərt) *v*. If you comfort someone, you say or do things to make the person feel better. When Jin's best friend moved away, her mom tried to comfort her.

command (kə·**mănd′**) *n*. If you do something on command, you do it because you were told to. When the trainer gave the command to stay, the dog immediately sat.

confidence (**kŏn′**·fī·dəns) *n*. If you have confidence, you have strong and sure feelings about yourself. Joe has confidence in his ability to do well in the cooking contest.

confront (kən·**frŭnt′**) *v*. When you confront a problem, you deal with that problem. It takes courage to confront a difficult situation.

considered (kən·**sĭd′**·ərd) *v*. If you considered something, you thought about it carefully. Meghan considered the teacher's question carefully before giving her answer.

consumed (kən·**sōomd′**) *v*. If you consumed something, you ate it. On our picnic, we consumed some of our favorite foods.

coveted (**kŭv′**·ĭ·tĭd) *v*. If you coveted something, you wanted it very much. Miguel had coveted a pet for so long, and now he has one.

creativity (**krē′**·ā·tĭv′·ĭ·tē) *n*. If someone has creativity, they are inventive, especially in the arts. Aunt Jillian's paintings show her creativity as an artist.

cruising (**krōoz′**·ĭng) *v*. If you are cruising, you are traveling in a boat for fun. We are cruising around the lake in our canoe.

curator (kyŏŏ·**rā′**·tər) *n*. A curator is the person who is in charge of the works of art or objects in a museum. My uncle is a curator at a large art museum in New York.

ă rat / ā pay / â care / ä father / ĕ pet / ē be / ĭ pit / ī pie / î fierce / ŏ pot / ō go / ô paw / ôr for / oi oil / ŏŏ book /

cynic (**sĭn′**•ĭk) *n.* A cynic is someone who always expects bad things to happen. Everyone was looking forward to the field trip, but as a cynic, Hannah was not so sure.

D

damp (dămp) *adj.* If something is damp, it feels a little wet. Mom asked me to move the load of damp clothes from the washing machine into the dryer.

dauntless (**dônt′**•lĭs) *adj.* Someone who is dauntless has no fears. The dauntless firefighter ran into the burning house to save the family.

debris (də•**brē′**) *n.* Debris is the pieces of something that was broken or destroyed. The people of the town had to work hard to clean up the debris that was left behind by the damaging hurricane.

Word Origins

debris The word *debris* is from the Old French word *débrisier,* which means "to break to pieces."

---

dedication (dĕd′•ĭ•**kā′**•shən) *n.* If someone has dedication for something, that person has shown commitment to it. Maria spends every weekend cleaning up the park, showing her dedication to her community.

defiance (dĭ•**fī′**•əns) *n.* If you act in defiance, you know something is not allowed, but you do it anyway. In an act of defiance, Buddy refused to come when I called him.

denying (dĭ•**nī′**•ĭng) *v.* Denying something means not believing that it's true. The children had a difficult time denying the fact that they were the ones who had broken the window.

descended (dĭ•**sĕn′**•dĭd) *v.* If something descended, it moved downwards. As the skydiver descended through the air, the open parachute looked like a beautiful rainbow.

despised (dĭ•**spīzd′**) *v.* If you despised something, you felt a strong dislike for it. Michael despised cold weather and shoveling snow.

destiny (**dĕs′**•tə•nē) *n.* A person's destiny is what will eventually happen in his or her life. Graduating from college was my destiny.

devised (dĭ•**vīzd′**) *v.* If you devised a plan, you figured out a way to achieve that plan. Our class devised a plan to build our own model of the solar system.

dignified (**dĭg′**•nə•fīd′) *adj.* If you are dignified, you act in a way that is formal, calm, and proper. The colonel acted in a dignified manner when speaking to the group about veterans and the importance of the military.

disbelief (dĭs′•bĭ•**lēf′**) *n.* Disbelief is not believing that something is true. The family was in disbelief when they heard the news.

ōō b**oo**t / ou **ou**t / ŭ c**u**t / û f**u**r / hw **wh**ich / th **th**in / th **th**is / zh vi**s**ion / ə **a**go, sil**e**nt, penc**i**l, lem**o**n, circ**u**s

disdain (dĭs•dān′) *n.* If you treat someone with disdain, you act as if he or she is unimportant or not as good as you are. When losing a game, you should always congratulate your opponent instead of treating them with disdain.

disheveled (dĭ•shĕv′•əld) *adj.* If something is disheveled, it is not neat or tidy. A disheveled room is messy and disorganized.

distant (dĭs′•tənt) *adj.* If something is distant, it is far away. As Malik stared towards the distant ocean, he was surprised by the sight of a group of dolphins jumping high into the air.

distinctive (dĭ•stĭngk′•tĭv) *adj.* If something is distinctive, it stands out in a way that makes it different or unusual. The umbrella was distinctive because of its bright yellow color.

distinguish (dĭ•stĭng′•gwĭsh) *v.* If you notice how things are different, you can distinguish them from one another. I can distinguish the two puppies from one another because only one has a white spot on his chest.

distress (dĭ•strĕs′) *n.* If you are in distress, you are very worried and upset. The loudly meowing cat seemed to be in distress.

doubts (douts) *n.* If you have doubts, you aren't sure about something. Aaron had doubts that the information was correct.

> **Word Origins**
>
> **doubts** The word *doubts* comes from the Latin word *dubtiare,* meaning "hesitant."

drifting (drĭf′•tĭng) *v.* If you are drifting, you are moving slowly without much direction. While we were scuba diving, we saw a plastic bag slowly drifting above the reef.

E

elaborately (ĭ•lăb′•ər•ĭt′•lē) *adv.* If something is elaborately dressed or decorated, it has many complex artistic details. The palace was elaborately built and decorated with gold.

elegant (ĕl′•ĭ•gənt) *adj.* Someone or something that is elegant is stylish and pleasant to look at. My aunt looked very elegant in her wedding dress.

endeavor (ĕn•dĕv′•ər) *v.* If you endeavor to do something, you try very hard to do it. Joon and Juan endeavor to finish the group project before it's due.

endurance (ĕn•dŏŏr′•əns) *n.* If you have endurance, you can do something for a long time. Running marathons requires endurance and strength.

ă r**a**t / ā p**ay** / â c**a**re / ä f**a**ther / ĕ p**e**t / ē b**e** / ĭ p**i**t / ī p**ie** / î f**ie**rce / ŏ p**o**t / ō g**o** / ô p**aw** / ôr f**or** / oi **oi**l / ŏŏ b**oo**k /

enhance (ĕn•**hăns'**) *v.* If you enhance something, you've made it into something better or improved upon it. Jessie worked hard to enhance her robot, in hopes of winning a prize at the school science fair.

episode (**ĕp'**•ĭ•sōd') *n.* An episode is an event or period of time that is important in some way. The day they broke the school record for tennis was the most memorable episode in their lives so far.

experience (ĭk•**spîr'**•ē•əns) *n.* Your experience is made up of past events and feelings. Meeting my favorite author is an experience I will never forget.

expressive (ĭk•**sprĕs'**•ĭv) *adj.* Someone who is expressive is clearly showing his or her feelings. The pianist's face was expressive during her solo performance.

extraordinarily (ĭk•**strôr'**•dn•âr'•ə•lē) *adv.* If something is done extraordinarily, it is very unusual or remarkable in some way. Liang is an extraordinarily skilled musician, as he is able to play many different instruments.

F

familiar (fə•**mĭl'**•yər) *adj.* Something familiar is something that you know and are used to. I see my familiar face looking back at me in the mirror.

fearlessness (**fîr'**•lĭs•nĭs) *n.* Having fearlessness in a situation means that you are not scared and feel brave. Climbing the rock wall requires a certain level of fearlessness.

feisty (**fī'**•stē) *adj.* Someone who is feisty is bold, energetic, and determined. Elijah is a feisty soccer player who kicks every ball with the goal of scoring.

ferocious (fə•**rō'**•shəs) *adj.* Something that is ferocious is very fierce, mean, and violent. The ferocious animal bared his teeth from on top of the rock.

flattered (**flăt'**•ərd) *adj.* If you are flattered by something, it made you feel honored or special. My mom was surprised and flattered by the special birthday card that I made for her.

foreboding (fôr•**bō'**•dĭng) *adj.* If something is described as foreboding, it suggests that something bad is going to happen. There were foreboding dark clouds that quickly rolled in from the west.

foreground (**fôr'**•ground') *n.* The foreground of a picture or photograph is the area that is closest to the viewer. In the photograph, the palm trees are visible in the foreground.

ōō b**oo**t / ou **ou**t / ŭ c**u**t / û f**u**r / hw **wh**ich / th **th**in / *th* **th**is / zh vi**si**on / ə **a**go, sil**e**nt, penc**i**l, lem**o**n, circ**u**s

forfeit (fôr′•fĭt) *v.* If you forfeit something, you lose it because you have broken a rule. We had to forfeit the game because we did not have enough players.

furious (fyo͝or′•ē•əs) *adj.* Someone who is furious is very, very angry. When you feel furious, it's a good idea to take a break and count to ten.

H

heritage (hĕr′•ĭ•tĭj) *n.* or *adj.* A person's heritage is the beliefs and traditions passed down from the people who lived before him or her. Each country has certain foods that reflect its heritage.

highlight (hī′•līt′) *v.* When you highlight something, you call attention to it. Paula will highlight the important information in her class notes with a yellow marker.

hilarious (hĭ•lâr′•ē•əs) *adj.* If something is hilarious, it is very funny. The movie was so hilarious that we laughed the entire time.

--- **Word Origins** ---

hilarious The word *hilarious* is from the Greek word *hilaros*, which means "cheerful."

hoard (hôrd) *n.* A hoard is a group of valuable things that is usually kept secret and carefully guarded by someone. My favorite book is about a dragon who guards a hoard of golden coins and jewels.

horizontal (hôr′•ĭ•zŏn′•tl) *adj.* If something is horizontal, it is level with the ground. The arrow was pointing in a horizontal direction.

I

identity (ī•dĕn′•tĭ•tē) *n.* Your identity is who you are. My love of sports is part of my identity.

illuminates (ĭ•lo͞o′•mə•nāts′) *v.* Something that illuminates gives off light and makes the area around it brighter. A lighthouse illuminates the water to guide approaching boats at night.

immigration (ĭm′•ĭ•grā′•shən) *n.* Immigration is the process of coming to live in a new country. Immigration workers make sure that people follow the laws about moving. People from all over the world have become United States citizens through the process of immigration.

inadvertently (ĭn′•əd•vûr′•tnt•lē) *adv.* If you act inadvertently, you do something by mistake or without realizing it. Josh was in such a hurry that he inadvertently wore two different shoes and socks to school.

inspiration (ĭn′•spə•rā′•shən) *n.* If you have an inspiration, you have an excited feeling that gives you new and creative ideas. One inspiration of mine is my brother, who taught me how to dance.

ă r**at** / ā p**ay** / â c**are** / ä f**ather** / ĕ p**et** / ē b**e** / ĭ p**it** / ī p**ie** / î f**ie**rce / ŏ p**ot** / ō g**o** / ô p**aw** / ôr f**or** / oi **oi**l / o͞o b**oo**k /

intimidated (ĭn•**tĭm′**•ĭ•dā′•tĭd) *v.*
Someone who is intimidated feels
afraid of someone or something.
We were intimidated by the look
on the tiger's face while at the zoo.

J

judge (jŭj) *v.* If you judge, you
guess or estimate the size or
amount of something. Patrick was
able to judge that he was about
two inches shorter than his brother.

> **Word Origins**
>
> **judge** The word *judge* comes
> from the Anglo-Norman word
> *juger*, meaning "one who
> makes estimates."

L

luminous (**lōo′**•mə•nəs) *adj.* If
something is luminous, it gives off
light. The luminous glow from the
flashlight allowed me to read while
we were camping.

M

majestic (mə•**jĕs′**•tĭk) *adj.*
Something that is majestic is
impressive and beautiful. The
hikers were amazed by the beauty
of the majestic mountains.

marveled (**mär′**•vəld) *v.* If you
marveled at something, you felt
surprised or amazed by it. We
marveled at the beauty of the
huge rainbow that appeared after
the thunderstorm.

mighty (**mī′**•tē) *adj.* Something
that is mighty is strong and
powerful. When we were at the
zoo last week, I heard the lion give
a loud and mighty roar.

mortal (**môr′**•tl) *n.* A mortal is a
person who lives and dies. In
myths, gods are not mortal
because they live forever. Each
human living on the Earth is
a mortal.

mundane (mŭn•**dān′**) *adj.*
Someone who is mundane is
ordinary and often dull. The
guest speaker was so mundane
that Rose nearly fell asleep during
the presentation.

N

necessary (**nĕs′**•ĭ•sĕr′•ē) *adj.*
If something is necessary, it is
needed, and you can't do without
it. Eating a well-balanced meal
is necessary for growing and
maintaining a strong and
healthy body.

> **Word Origins**
>
> **necessary** The word
> *necessary* is from the Latin
> word *necesse*, which means
> "be needful."

O

obliged (ə•**blījd′**) *v.* If you obliged,
you did what you were asked or
expected to do. When his father
asked him to wash the dishes,
Calvin obliged.

ōō b**oo**t / ou **ou**t / ŭ c**u**t / û f**u**r / hw **wh**ich / th **th**in / *th* **th**is / zh vi**si**on / ə **a**go, sil**e**nt, penc**i**l, lem**o**n, circ**u**s

observant (əb•**zûr′**•vənt) *adj.* If you are observant, you see or notice more details than other people. My grandmother is very observant, so she shows me the finer details of the quilt.

obstacles (**ŏb′**•stə•kəlz) *n.* Obstacles are objects that make it hard to get where you want to go. We ran through obstacles in gym class.

occasionally (ə•**kā′**•zhə•nə•lē) *adv.* If you do something occasionally, you do it only once in awhile. We would occasionally see a shooting star while we were camping.

odyssey (**ŏd′**•ĭ•sē) *n.* An odyssey is a long journey that is exciting and eventful. We used a map to plan our odyssey around the world.

─── **Word Origins** ───
odyssey The word *odyssey* is from Homer's poem about the adventures of the Greek warrior Odysseus.

opportunities (ŏp′•ər•**tōō′**•nĭ•tēz) *n.* If you have opportunities, you have chances to make something good happen. Mrs. Gregor gives us many opportunities to solve problems on our own.

P

perception (pər•**sĕp′**•shən) *n.* Your perception of something is how you notice or experience it using your senses. The amount of light in a room affects our perception of the objects in it.

perished (**pĕr′**•ĭshd) *v.* When people or animals perished, they died. Many plants in the area perished from the extreme drought.

plunges (**plŭn**•jĕs) *v.* If something plunges into something, it falls or is thrown in that direction. The mountain river plunges to the rocks below, creating a beautiful waterfall.

polished (**pŏl′**•ĭsht) *adj.* A performance that is polished is given with great skill and no mistakes. Julia practiced for hours so she could give a polished performance on the ice rink.

proclaimed (prə•**klāmd′**) *v.* If you proclaimed something, you said it in a strong way to show it was important for others to hear. In the middle of dinner, Matthew proclaimed the good news that he had won the spelling bee.

profound (prə•**found′**) *adj.* A profound thought is one that is deep and meaningful. After Jayden read his essay, his profound thoughts started a class discussion.

pursuit (pər•**sōōt′**) *n.* A pursuit is something you attempt to accomplish. In pursuit of the science fair trophy, we worked after school every day for a month.

─── **Word Origins** ───
pursuit The word *pursuit* is from the Old French word *porsuite*, which means "a search."

ă **r**at / ā **pay** / â **c**are / ä **f**ather / ĕ **pet** / ē **be** / ĭ **pit** / ī **pie** / î **fie**rce / ŏ **pot** / ō **go** / ô **paw** / ôr **for** / oi **oil** / ŏŏ **book** /

R

rebellion (rĭ·**bĕl′**·yən) *n.* In a rebellion, people defy authority and fight for change in their political system. Throughout history, there have been many times when rebellion has brought about change.

reflect (rĭ·**flĕkt′**) *v.* When light reflects off a surface, it bounces back without passing through the surface. As the sun went down, the surface of the lake was able to reflect the colors of the sunset.

refugees (rĕf′·yŏŏ·**jēz′**) *n.* Refugees are people who must leave their countries because of war or other serious problems. Some refugees who flee their homeland must start new lives in a different country.

regretted (rĭ·**grĕt′**·tĭd) *v.* If you regretted something, you felt sorry about it and wished you hadn't done it. I regretted letting my dog play with the stuffed animal.

relish (**rĕl′**·ĭsh) *v.* If you relish something, you enjoy it very much. I relish the chance to watch your dog while you are on vacation!

relying (rĭ·**lī′**·ĭng) *v.* When you are relying on someone, you are trusting or depending on that person. The people of the community are relying on the police officers to make their neighborhood a safe place to live.

resolutions (rĕz′·ə·**lōō′**·shənz) *n.* Resolutions are promises to do or not do something. One of my resolutions is to eat a vegetable every day.

rhythmic (**rĭ***th***′**·mĭk) *adj.* If something is rhythmic, it has a pattern of sounds, movements, or beats that repeat. The rhythmic pattern of the drums helped the band stay in step as they marched in the parade.

rigid (**rĭj′**·ĭd) *adj.* Something that is rigid is stiff and does not bend easily. The gymnast held her body in a rigid pose as she practiced her routine.

S

savor (**sā′**·vər) *v.* If you savor something, you take your time enjoying it. William ate slowly so that he could savor every bite of the delicious meal.

scowled (skould) *v.* If you scowled, you frowned or had an angry look on your face. If a person scowled, it probably meant that he or she was not very happy about something.

sculpture (**skŭlp′**·chər) *n.* A sculpture is something that a person creates by shaping or carving things like clay, stone, or wood. The clay sculpture that won first prize in the art contest was placed at the front of the classroom.

ōō b**oo**t / ou **ou**t / ŭ c**u**t / û f**u**r / hw **wh**ich / th **th**in / *th* **th**is / zh vi**s**ion / ə **a**go, sil**e**nt, penc**i**l, lem**o**n, circ**u**s

secure (sĭ·**kyŏor'**) *v.* When you secure an area, you make it safe from being attacked. The castle had high walls to secure it from attack.

spare (spâr) *v.* Something you can spare is something extra that you have and that you don't really need. Brenna had a strip of paper to spare, so she gave it to Max.

spectators (**spĕk'**·tā'·tərz) *n.* Spectators are people who watch an event, such as a sports competition. The spectators at the baseball game watched intently.

stir (stûr) *n.* If you cause a stir, you create a strong feeling, such as excitement or shock. It caused a stir when the principal announced the plans for a new playground.

strenuous (**strĕn'**·yōo·əs) *adj.* If an activity is strenuous, it takes great effort or a lot of energy. The most strenuous part of the trip was carrying my thirty-five pound backpack up the mountain.

stunned (stŭnd) *adj.* If you are stunned, you are shocked or amazed by something. They were stunned at the end of the movie.

subdued (səb·**dōod'**) *adj.* Something that is subdued is quiet and low key. Aunt Helen answered her phone in a subdued voice, so she would not wake the sleeping baby.

sulked (sŭlkd) *v.* If you sulked, you were crabby because you were annoyed or disappointed about something. Melissa sulked in her room when she saw that it was raining outside.

sumptuous (**sŭmp'**·chōo·əs) *adj.* Something that is sumptuous is impressive and expensive-looking. Royalty will often live in large and sumptuous palaces that are filled with beautiful furnishings.

surge (sûrj) *n.* If there is a surge of water, there is a sudden large increase in its depth. A surge of water rose onto the concrete landing below our house.

surrendered (sə·**rĕn'**·dərd) *v.* If you surrendered to an enemy, you gave up and agreed that the other side won. Audrey surrendered right before Wes was about to throw another snowball at her.

T

tactile (**tăk'**·təl) *adj.* Something that is tactile is experienced through the sense of touch. Petting a dog is a tactile experience.

taunt (tônt) *n.* A taunt is something someone says to anger or upset someone else. During a competition, opponents may yell a taunt at each other.

timid (**tĭm'**·ĭd) *adj.* If you are timid, you are very careful and often fearful. The timid cat would not come off the couch.

ă r**at** / ā p**ay** / â c**are** / ä f**a**ther / ĕ p**e**t / ē b**e** / ĭ p**i**t / ī p**ie** / î f**ie**rce / ŏ p**o**t / ō g**o** / ô p**aw** / ôr f**or** / oi **oi**l / ōo b**oo**k /

trampled (**trăm′**•pəld) *v.* If something is trampled, it is stepped on and damaged or crushed. Robert trampled the flowers as he walked through the garden.

transparent (trăns•**pâr′**•ənt) *adj.* If an object is transparent, you can see through it. When I look through the transparent glass walls of the aquarium, I can see guppies.

trickle (**trĭk′**•əl) *n.* A trickle is a small amount of slowly flowing water. During the summer when there is not much rain, a large waterfall can slow to a trickle.

tyrant (**tī′**•rənt) *n.* A tyrant is a powerful person who rules others in a cruel or unreasonable way. The king was a mighty tyrant who never allowed his subjects to leave the kingdom.

U

unsurpassed (ŭn′•sĕr•**păst′**) *v.* If something is unsurpassed, there is nothing that is better. In my opinion, the beauty of a sunset over an ocean is unsurpassed.

V

verses (vûrs•əs) *n.* The verses of a song are the different sections that usually change throughout the song. We had to memorize all the verses of the song for the music competition.

W

wisdom (**wĭz′**•dəm) *n.* If you have wisdom, you are able to use your experience to make good decisions. Our grandmother, who is full of wisdom, always gives us good advice.

ōō b**oo**t / ou **ou**t / ŭ c**u**t / û f**u**r / hw **wh**ich / th **th**in / *th* **th**is / zh vi**s**ion / ə **a**go, sil**e**nt, penc**i**l, lem**o**n, circ**u**s

Index of Titles and Authors

Acknowledgments

"Balloon" from *Wet Cement: A Mix of Concrete Poems* by Bob Raczka. Copyright © 2016 by Bob Raczka. Reprinted by permission of Roaring Brook Press, a division of Holtzbrinck Publishing Holdings Limited Partnership.

The Battle of the Alamo by Amie Jane Leavitt. Copyright © 2008 by Capstone Press. Reprinted by permission of Capstone Press Publishers.

The Beatles Were Fab (and They Were Funny) by Kathleen Krull and Paul Brewer, illustrated by Stacy Innerts. Text copyright © 2013 by Kathleen Krull and Paul Brewer. Illustrations © by Stacy Innerts. Reprinted by permission of Houghton Mifflin Harcourt Publishing Company.

"Better Fun" from *Animal Poems of the Iguazu* by Francisco X. Alarcón. Text copyright © 2008 by Francisco X. Alarcón. Reprinted by permission of Children's Book Press, an imprint of Lee & Low Books Inc.

"Blind Ambition" by Matthew Cooper and Rachel Buchholz, illustrated by Karine Aigner, from *National Geographic Kids,* November 2008. Copyright © 2008 by the National Geographic Society. Reprinted by permission of the National Geographic Society.

Excerpt from *Catch Me If You Can* by Carol Schaffner. Text copyright © 2015 by Plays Magazine. Reprinted by permission of *Plays, The Drama Magazine for Young People*/Sterling Partners, Inc.

Excerpt from *The Devil and Miss Prym* by Paulo Coelho. Text copyright © 2000 by Paulo Coelho. English translation copyright © 2000 by Amanca Hopkinson and Nick Caistor. Reprinted by permission of HarperCollins Publishers.

Excerpt from *Flora & Ulysses: The Illuminated Adventures* by Kate DiCamillo, illustrated by K. G. Campbell. Text copyright © 2013 by Kate DiCamillo. Illustrations copyright © 2013 by K. G. Campbell. Reprinted by permission of Candlewick Press and Penguin Random House Audio Publishing Group, a division of Penguin Random House LLC.

Excerpt from *The Game of Silence* by Louise Erdrich. Text copyright © 2005 by Louise Erdrich. Reprinted by permission of HarperCollins Publishers.

Kitoto the Mighty by Tololwa M. Mollel, illustrated by Kristi Frost. Text copyright © 1998 by Tololwa M. Mollel. Illustrations copyright © 1998 by Kristi Frost. Published 1998 by Stoddart Kids. Reprinted by permission of Fitzhenry & Whiteside, Markham, Ontario, Canada.

"Let's Dance Around the World" (retitled from: "Hip-Hop, Rap-a-Tap, Let's Dance Around the World") by Leticia Ann Kumura and Annabel Wildrick, illustrated by Patty Weise from *AppleSeeds Magazine,* May 2004. Text copyright © 2004 by Carus Publishing Company. Reprinted by permission of Cricket Media. All Cricket Media material is copyrighted by Carus Publishing d/b/a Cricket Media, and/or various authors and illustrators. Any commercial use or distribution of material without permission is strictly prohibited. Please visit http://www.cricketmedia.com/info/licensing2 for licensing and http://www.cricketmedia.com for subscriptions.

My Diary from Here to There by Amada Irma Pérez, illustrated by Maya Christina González. Text copyright © 2002 by Amada Irma Pérez. Illustrations copyright © 2002 by Maya Christina González. Reprinted by permission of Children's Book Press, an imprint of Lee & Low Books Inc.

"The Big-Word Girl", "Eating Alphabet Soup", and "Necessary Gardens" from *Please Bury Me in the Library* by J. Patrick Lewis. Text copyright © 2005 by J. Patrick Lewis. Reprinted by permission of Houghton Mifflin Harcourt Publishing Company.

Excerpt from "One on one interview: 'John Carter's' Lynn Collins" by Steven Lebowitz from Examiner.com, March 11, 2012. Text copyright © 2012 by Steven Lebowitz. Reprinted by permission of Steven Lebowitz.

"Prince Charming Misplaces His Bride" (excerpted and titled from *The Hero's Guide to Saving Your Kingdom*) by Christopher Healy, illustrated by Todd Harris. Text copyright © 2012 by Christopher Healy. Reprinted by permission of HarperCollins Publishers.

"Quiet Water" from *Animal Poems of the Iguazú* by Francisco X. Alarcón. Text copyright © 2008 by Francisco X. Alarcón. Reprinted by permission of Children's Book Press, an imprint of Lee & Low Books Inc.

Rent Party Jazz by William Miller, illustrated by Charlotte Riley-Webb. Text copyright © 2001 by William Miller. Illustrations copyright © 2001 by Charlotte Riley-Webb. Reprinted by permission of Lee & Low Books Inc.

Credits